# Mata Vaishno Devi

# Mata Vaishno Devi

*The Bhakti of Shakti*

RUPA

First published by
Rupa Publications India Pvt. Ltd 2023
7/16, Ansari Road, Daryaganj
New Delhi 110002

*Sales Centres:*
Bengaluru Chennai
Hyderabad Jaipur Kathmandu
Kolkata Mumbai Prayagraj



P-ISBN: 978-93-5702-578-2
E-ISBN: 978-93-5702-579-9

First impression 2023

10 9 8 7 6 5 4 3 2 1

# Contents

# Introduction

One of the places synonymous with pilgrimage and the Hindu faith, alongside Kedarnath and Kashi, is the holy shrine of Shri Mata Vaishno Devi Ji. Every year, millions of devotees make the 12-km trek from the base camp in Katra to reach the holy cave and pay obeisance to the benevolent deity that resides there.

As a mark of the devotee's fervour, a silver coin bearing the mark of the goddess is given. The coin is one of the most memorable and well-known parts of the pilgrimage, known even to those who have not had the opportunity to be graced by the Mata's presence. This pilgrimage is considered to be one of the holiest pilgrimages a devotee can undertake.

To understand and go into more detail regarding this most powerful and holiest of shrines, one needs to understand the history and faith of Mata Vaishno Devi Ji and how the shrine came to be discovered by mortals and worshipped in the form that it is today.

Vaishno Devi Temple

ONE

# The Devi

# Who Is Vaishno Devi?

Mata Vaishno Devi is also widely known as Mata Rani, Trikuta, Ambe or Vaishnavi. She is considered to be a manifestation of the Hindu Mother Goddess Shakti. In addition to this, some also believe that Mata Vaishno Devi possesses the powers of the Hindu God Vishnu, and hence, she is called Vaishno Devi.

According to legends, during the time of great disorder and chaos, when asuras were roaming the earth and wreaking havoc upon innocent people and their lives, Shakti appeared to protect the weak and the defenceless. She vanquished the asuras and made them fear her. But the earth was overrun by them, and Shakti could not be everywhere. To cover every blade of grass and every bit of the earth, she created three manifestations, each with terrifying and destructive power. These manifestations were Maha Kali, Maha Lakshmi and Maha Saraswati. The three manifestations hounded the asuras and protected people all over the world.

The Three Manifestations of Shakti

However, there was still something remaining. Shakti and her three manifestations could see that upholding righteousness and spreading devotion could not be accomplished simply by fighting and defeating asuras. The people and devotees needed someone to look up to and take inspiration from.

The three devis, then, decided to concentrate their energies and powers together. From their collective strength and power (*tejas*), a young girl emerged and asked the three manifestations of Shakti about her purpose and goal. The devis told the girl that she was to be the shining light to lead humanity into an age of peace and devotion, and that she was to uphold the righteousness that had been damaged by the continuous desecration of the asuras. Thus, Vaishno Devi took shape and was born among humans.

From here on, there are a few legends that tell different stories towards the origin of the Vaishno Devi shrine and the Devi herself.

The most prominent legend maintains that in the Treta Yuga, a beautiful girl child was born to Ratankar, a simple farmer living in southern India, and his wife. The couple named the child Vaishnavi, as they believed that she was a part of Vishnu. Right from her early years, Vaishnavi displayed a hunger for knowledge, which no amount of reading, writing or explaining could satisfy. Subsequently, she started looking inwards for knowledge and soon learnt meditation. She realized that it was the only way through which she could bring herself close to her objective of attaining more knowledge and wisdom. Vaishnavi thus relinquished all kinds of luxuries and went deep into the forest near Rameswaram to meditate. There, she cultivated knowledge and focussed her meditation upon Lord Rama.

Lord Rama, during his 14 years of exile in the forest under the orders of his father King Dusratha, happened to visit Vaishnavi, who immediately recognized him. She sensed that Rama was no ordinary being but an incarnation of Lord Vishnu. Thus, she pleaded with him to let her merge into him so that she could become one with the preserver. However, Lord Rama, knowing that it was not the appropriate time to do so, said that he would visit her again after the end of his exile, and if she succeeded in recognizing him then, he would grant her wish and allow her to merge into him.

True to his word, Lord Rama visited Vaishnavi again after being victorious in the battle against Ravana, having finished his exile and retaken the throne at Ayodhya. But this time, he disguised himself as an old man. Unfortunately, Vaishnavi was unable to recognize him and was distraught when he revealed himself. Lord Rama consoled her by saying that the appropriate time for her being one with the preserver had not come yet, and that a time would come eventually during the 'Kalyug' when Vishnu would be in his tenth incarnation of 'Kalki'. This was when Vaishnavi would merge into Vishnu. Lord Rama tasked Vaishnavi with meditation, and to set up an ashram at the base of Trikuta Hill, so that she could elevate her spirituality, bless mankind, and rid the poor and destitute of their sufferings and give them some respite and joy. After she had completed these tasks, she could merge with Vishnu. Thus, Vaishnavi set off for the north, and after a lot of hardships and challenges, reached the foot of the Trikuta Hill. There, she set up her ashram as instructed by Lord Rama and began to meditate with utmost devotion.

As predicted by Lord Rama, Vaishnavi's glory spread and people began to flock to her ashram to seek her blessings. As her fame spread, Mahayogi Guru Goraksh Nath, who had a vision of the rendezvous between Lord Rama and Vaishnavi, became curious to find out whether she had attained a high level of spirituality. Therefore, Guru Goraksh Nath sent his most trusted disciple Bhairon Nath to find out the truth. Upon locating the ashram, Bhairon Nath started spying on Vaishnavi and realized that though she was a *sadhvi*, she always carried weapons with her and was always surrounded by langurs and a ferocious lion. Bhairon Nath was enamored by Vaishnavi's extraordinary beauty, and losing all sense of decorum, he began to harass Vaishnavi to marry him.

Pandit Sridhar, one of Vaishnavi's most ardent devotees who lived nearby, organized a *bhandara* in which the entire village as well as Guru Goraksh Nath and his followers were invited. During the course of the bhandara, Bhairon Nath, in the throes of lust, attempted to grab Vaishnavi. She evaded him but could not continue to keep doing so. Therefore, she decided to flee into the mountains to continue her *tapasaya* undisturbed and away from the lascivious eyes of Bhairon Nath. He, however, followed her to her destination.

After halting at Banganga, Charan Paduka and Adhkuwari, Vaishnavi finally reached the holy cave. When Bhairon Nath continued to follow her despite her attempts to avoid any kind of confrontation, she had to kill him, as he would have kept interrupting her meditation, which was the duty given to her by Vishnu. Bhairon Nath met his end just outside the cave, where the goddess decapitated him. The severed head of the former disciple of Goraksh Nath fell with force at a distant hilltop. Only upon death did Bhairon Nath realize the futility of his desire and prayed to the deity he had wronged to forgive him. The almighty Mata had mercy on him and blessed him with a sanctum in the shrine of Shri Mata Vaishno Devi, which is revered by everyone.

Another legend states that after accepting Lord Rama's advice and proceeding to Trikuta, Vaishanavi found out that the hill was under the sway of a demon named Bhairon. Upon seeing her, Bhairon was bewitched by her beauty and wanted to possess her. Vaishnavi tried to escape and took a dangerous route to the mountain in order to dodge Bhairon. On her way there, several people saw the glow of divinity upon her and started following her in devotion.

Upon reaching Banganga, the devotees felt parched and thirsty. Not a drop of water could be found. Acknowledging their faith and the problem, Vaishno Devi invoked her divine powers and shot an arrow into a nearby rock. A pure stream of water flowed out, and it was given the name 'Banganga', which means Ganga that flows out due to an arrow being launched.

Vaishno Devi, concerned for her devotees and wishing to avoid Bhairon, left them at Banganga and continued her climb alone. She stopped for a short while at a place, which is now called Charan Paduka, where she looked back to see if the demon was still following her. The rock on which she stood and steeled herself bear the imprints of her feet, which can still be seen to this day, and a temple commemorating them has been erected there.

When Vaishno Devi reached Adhkuwari, she went inside a cave and meditated there for a period of nine months. Bhairon, all this while, had been following her. After a long time, he managed to locate Vaishno Devi. He reached the mouth of the cave and blocked all avenues of escape for the goddess. A mendicant nearby, recognizing Vaishno Devi as Shakti, warned Bhairon to give up his fruitless endeavour. Overtaken by lust, Bhairon did not waver. As he moved towards her, Vaishno Devi, using her divine strength, cut up the rock behind her and escaped through an opening in between them. This small niche in the rock is known as Garbh Joon.

Upon escaping the cave, Vaishno Devi took a yet steeper path, which is known as 'Hathi-Matha', since it resembles the forehead of an elephant. From there, she reached the main cave, but Bhairon was still in pursuit. Realizing that there was no stopping him and his lust, Vaishno Devi assumed her divine form as Shakti and emerged from her cave, dressed in bright red clothes and riding a lion. She held weapons in each of her eight hands, and hurled a *trishul* (trident) at Bhairon. The force of the throw severed Bhairon's head, which fell almost 1.4 km away, in a place today known as Bhairon Ghati. His torso remained rooted to the cave, and it can be seen today as a boulder at the cave entrance.

As he lay dying, Bhairon repented and begged the goddess to forgive him and bless him so that his body would remain where it was and that people would encounter his remains while they were on a pilgrimage to Vaishno Devi. The goddess granted this wish, and it was in fulfilment of this wish that she ensured that the devotees, while doing *darshan,* did not walk over the body of Bhairon. It was so positioned that the pilgrims had to crawl over the curves of the cave wall before they could come face to face with the three pindis.

Yet another version of the legend maintains that at the time of Vaishnavi's human existence, a king by the name of Bhairon Bali ruled the area between Sutlej and Jhelum. He was a tyrant who had no mercy for his subjects. Those who were oppressed by him prayed to Vaishno Devi and approached her hermitage to save them from his misrule. Vaishno Devi agreed to help and came down from her abode in Trikuta Hill to organize a gathering of the aggrieved villagers and chart out a plan. The tyrant king showed up to the gathering, intending to punish his subjects and abduct Vaishno Devi so that he could marry her. Since Vaishno Devi was the goddess incarnate, she knew she could not be caught. She proceeded towards her cave, and on the way, organized rebellions that freed Bhairon Bali's oppressed subjects. The tyrant tried to give her a chase but was struck down by her trident much in the same way as in the other tellings of the legend.

Another set of myths places Vaishno Devi in each

of the four Yugas. In the Sat Yuga, she appeared as the eldest of the seven sisters who were sent to the earth by the sages in the shape of seven goddesses. She took a mortal form to put an end to Mahishasura, who spread his evil throughout the world and put the existence of the universe in danger. After successfully destroying Mahishasura, order returned to the universe and everything was peaceful again. Here, Vaishno Devi is seen as one of the prime forces keeping chaos and demons at bay and helping peace prevail.

In the Dwapara Yuga, Vaishno Devi was known as the protector of truth and justice. The Mahabharata occurred in this Yuga, and Vaishno Devi finds a mention in the epic. Before heading towards the battlefield at Kurukshetra to fight against the Kauravas, Lord Krishna advised Arjuna that he should visit the hills of Jammu and seek Vaishno Devi's blessings. Arjuna agreed to this advice and visited Trikuta, where he worshipped the goddess.

## Where Does She Reside?

As with the most ancient and holiest of shrines, it is not possible to ascertain when exactly the pilgrimage to Vaishno Devi started. Early Vedic literature has no reference to the worship of any female deity in the region, although the mountain Trikuta does find a mention in the Rig Veda, the oldest of the four Vedas. The practice of worshipping Shakti, whose manifestation is Vaishno Devi, largely started during the Puranic period.

The first mention of Mahadevi is in the epic the Mahabharata. When the armies of Pandavas and Kauravas were arrayed in the battlefield of Kurukshetra, Arjuna, the chief warrior of Pandavas, upon the advice of Shri Krishna, meditated upon Mahadevi and sought her blessings for victory. This is when Arjuna addressed her as 'Jambookatak Chityaishu Nityam Sannihitalaye', which means 'you who always dwell in the temple on the slope of the mountain in Jamboo', with Jamboo probably referring to Jammu.

It is believed that the Pandavas were the first to build the temples at Kol Kandoli and Bhawan in reverence and gratitude towards Mahadevi. On a mountain adjacent to the Trikuta Hill and overlooking the holy cave are five stone structures, which are believed to be the rock symbols of the five Pandavas.

Some traditions believe this shrine to be the holiest of all Shakti Peethas, since the skull of Sati fell there. Others believe that her right arm fell there—in the holy cave of Shri Mata Vaishno Devi, one does find stone remains of a human hand, popularly known as Varad Hast (the hand that grants boons and blessings).

The Three Pindis

The Trikuta Hill, where the shrine is located, and the holy cave are the gateway to the dimension of super consciousness. Just like the Trikuta Hill, which is one at the base but has three peaks (hence, the name *trikoot*), the revelation of the Mother Goddess in the holy cave is in a natural rock form, which is one at the base but has three heads at the top. These three heads in a natural rock form are known as the holy pindis and are worshipped as Mahadevi. The entire rock body is immersed in water and a marble platform has now been constructed all around. The uniqueness of the holy pindis is that although they emanate from one single rock form, each one is different from the other two in colour and texture.

# The Three Pindis

## Maha Kali

Maha Kali, as Shakti,
Standing on the Inert Body of Shiva

Towards the right of where the devotees stand is the holy pindi of Mata Maha Kali (the Supreme Energy of Dissolution) in black. She represents the tamas *guna* (quality) and is associated with the darker and unknown realms of life. *Tam* stands for darkness. Before creation, there was darkness, and following creation or destruction, there is darkness again. While creation abounds around us, the realm of darkness is the realm of mystery. The energy of darkness, which transcends the barriers of time, is the Eternal Time or Maha Kali. Since man's knowledge about life is very limited and he remains in the dark about most of it, it is represented by the colour black, which is associated with Maha Kali. She is the source of all that is mystical and unknown to man. In her attribute of Maha Kali, Mahadevi guides her devotees to conquer the forces of darkness.

Maha Kali is most often depicted with blue/black complexion in popular Indian art. Her most common four-armed iconography shows each hand carrying a crescent-shaped sword, a trishul, a severed head of a demon and a bowl or skull-cup (*kapala*) catching the blood from the severed head. Her eyes are described as red with intoxication and absolute rage, her hair is shown to be dishevelled, small fangs sometimes protrude out of her mouth and her tongue is lolling. Having consumed the blood of the demons she has slayed, it drips off of her lolling tongue. She is adorned with a garland consisting of the heads of demons she has slaughtered, variously enumerated at 108 (an auspicious number in Hinduism and the number of countable beads on a *japa mala*, similar to a rosary, for repetition of mantras) or 50 (representing the number of letters in Devanagari) and wears a skirt made of demon arms.

Her *dashamukhi* (10-headed) image is known as the 10 Mahavidyas, and in this form, she is said to represent the 10 Mahavidyas or Great Wisdom (Goddesses). She is sometimes shown sitting on a flaming grave or a rotting corpse. Her complexion is described as that of the night sky, devoid of stars. She is depicted in this form as having 10 heads, 30 flaming eyes, 10 arms and 10 legs, but in other respects, usually conforms to the four-armed icon. Each of her 10 hands carries an implement, which differs across different accounts, but each of these represent the power of one of the devas, often being the identifying weapon or ritual item of a deva. The implication is that Maha Kali subsumes and is responsible for the powers these deities possess, and this is in line with the interpretation that Maha Kali is identical with the *brahman*. When not displaying 10 heads, an *ekamukhi* or one-headed image may be displayed with 10 arms, signifying the same concept: she is the source of the ten avatars of Vishnu, with each avatar corresponding to one of the 10 aspects of Maha Kali.

She is often shown standing on the prone, inert body of Shiva. This is interpreted in various ways, but the most common understanding is that Maha Kali represents

Shakti, the power of pure creation in the universe, and Shiva represents pure consciousness, which is inert. While this is an advanced concept in monistic Shaktism, it also agrees with the nondual Trika philosophy of Kashmir, popularly known as Kashmir Shaivism, and is associated most famously with a philosopher called Abhinavagupta. There is a colloquial saying that 'Shiva without Shakti is *shava*'. This means that without the power of action (shakti) that is Maha Kali, Shiva (consciousness) is inactive; 'shava' means corpse in Sanskrit. This is often the explanation for why she is standing on Shiva, who is her husband in Shaktism, and also the supreme godhead in Shaivism. Another understanding is that the wild, destructive Maha Kali can only stop her fury in the presence of Shiva, the god of consciousness, so that the balance of life is not overrun over by wild nature.

## Maha Lakshmi

In the centre is the holy pindi of Mata Maha Lakshmi (the Supreme Energy of Maintenance) with a yellowish-red tinge, the colour associated with Mata Maha Lakshmi. She represents the rajas guna as well as *iccha-shakti*. Her four arms are symbolic of the four goals of humanity that are considered good in Hinduism: dharma (pursuit of an ethical, moral life), artha (pursuit of wealth, means of life), kama (pursuit of love, emotional fulfilment) and moksha (pursuit of self-knowledge, liberation).

Maha Lakshmi in Her Classic
Iconography of the Lotus

Maha Lakshmi is usually shown as either sitting or standing on a lotus and typically carrying a lotus in one or two hands. The lotus symbolizes knowledge, self-realization and liberation, and represents reality, consciousness and karma in the Tantras (extensive ritual manual dating as early as seventh century and as late as the nineteenth century). The lotus, a flower that blooms in clean or dirty water, also symbolizes purity regardless of the good or bad circumstances of growth. It is a reminder that goodness and prosperity can bloom and not be affected by evil in one's surroundings.

Lakshmi Sahasranama of the Skanda Purana, Lakshmi Tantra, the Markandeya Purana, Devi Mahatmya and Vedic scriptures describe Maha Lakshmi as having 18 hands and holding a rosary, axe, mace, arrow, thunderbolt, lotus, pitcher, lance, cudgel, sword, shield, conch, bell, wine cup, trident, noose and discus in her hands.

Maha Lakshmi is very often shown surrounded by one or two elephants and is known as Gajalakshmi. She is occasionally depicted with an owl in the frame too. Elephants symbolize work, activity and strength, as well as water, rain and fertility for abundant prosperity. The owl signifies the patient striving to observe, see and discover knowledge, particularly when surrounded by darkness. As a bird reputedly blinded by daylight, the owl also serves as a symbolic reminder to refrain from blindness and greed after knowledge and wealth have been acquired. Mata Maha Lakshmi is *simhavahini* (mount as lion) on most of the coins during the Gupta rule. Coins during the rule of Prakashadiya, a Gupta ruler, are imprinted with the Garudadhvaja on the obverse and Lakshmi on the reverse. In the early iconography of Gupta period, lions used to be associated only with Lakshmi. Later, it also became a symbol of Durga. Lions are also associated with Veera Lakshmi, who is one of the Ashtalakshmi.

In some representations, wealth either symbolically pours out from one of her hands or she simply holds a jar of money. This symbolism has a dual meaning: wealth manifested through Lakshmi means both material as well as spiritual wealth. Her face and open hands are in a mudra that signifies compassion, giving or *dana* (charity).

Lakshmi typically wears a red dress embroidered with golden threads, which symbolizes fortune and wealth. She, goddess of wealth and prosperity, is often represented with her husband Vishnu, the god who maintains human life filled with justice and peace. This symbolism implies that wealth and prosperity are coupled with the maintenance of life, justice and peace.

### Maha Saraswati

The pindi to the extreme left of the viewer is worshipped as the holy pindi of Mata Maha Saraswati (the Supreme Energy of Creation). It has a whitish tinge when looked at attentively. White, as a colour denoting purity, has also been considered as the colour associated with Mata Maha Saraswati. Being the supreme force of creation, Mata Maha Saraswati is considered to be the source of all creation, knowledge, wisdom, righteousness, art, spiritualism, piousness, etc. She represents the sattva guna—the quality of purity.

Maha Saraswati, in Her Four-Armed
Avatar with Her Icon of the Peacock

Maha Saraswati is often depicted as dressed in pure white, often seated on a white lotus, which symbolizes light, knowledge and truth. She not only embodies knowledge but also the experience of the highest reality. She is typically shown in white themes—from her dress to flowers to swan—the colour symbolizing sattva guna. Her dhyana mantra describes her to be as white as the moon, clad in a white dress, bedecked in white ornaments, radiant with beauty, holding a book and a pen in her hands (the book represents knowledge).

She is generally shown to have four arms, but in some representations, she has just two. When shown with four hands, those hands symbolically mirror her husband Brahma's four heads, representing *manas* (mind, sense), *buddhi* (intellect, reasoning), *citta* (imagination, creativity) and *ahamkara* (self-consciousness, ego). Brahma represents the abstract while she represents action and reality.

The four hands hold items with symbolic meanings—a *pustaka* (book), a *mala*, a water pot and a *veena* (a stringed musical instrument). The book she holds symbolizes the Vedas, representing the universal, divine, eternal and true knowledge as well as all forms of learning. The mala of crystals represents the power of meditation, inner reflection and spirituality. The pot of water represents the purifying power to separate right from wrong, the clean from the unclean and essential from the inessential. In some texts, the pot of water is a symbol for *soma*—the drink that liberates and leads to knowledge. The most famous feature of Saraswati is the veena, which represents all creative arts, and her holding it symbolizes expressing knowledge that creates harmony. Saraswati is also associated with *anuraga*, the love for and rhythm of music, which represents all emotions and feelings expressed in speech or music.

A *hamsa*—either a swan or a goose—is often shown near her feet. In Hindu mythology, the hamsa is a sacred bird, which, if offered a mixture of milk and water, is said to be able to drink the milk alone. It, thus, symbolizes the ability to discriminate between good and evil, essence from the outward show and the eternal from the evanescent. Due to her association with the swan, Saraswati is also referred to as Hamsavahini, which means 'she who has a hamsa as her vehicle'. The hamsa is also a symbol of spiritual perfection, transcendence and moksha. Sometimes, a *citramekhala* (also called *mayura* or peacock) is shown beside the goddess. The peacock symbolizes colourful splendour, the celebration of dance and, as the devourer of snakes, the ability to transmute the serpent poison of ignorance into the radiant plumage of enlightenment.

## Mahadevi

Mahadevi, of whom Shri Mata Vaishno Devi Ji is considered a form, is known by many names. She is commonly known as Mulaprakrti (she who is primordial matter) and Mahamaya (she who is the great *maya*). The Devi Bhagavata Purana and Lalita Sahasranama describe Mahadevi's numerous epithets. These names include her divine and destructive characteristics. In the Devi Bhagavata Purana, she is described as 'the mother of all', 'the life force in all beings' and 'she who is supreme knowledge'. The Lalita Sahasranama also describes her as Visvadhika (she who transcends the universe), Sarvaga (she who is omnipresent), Vishvadharini (she who supports the universe), Rakshasaghni (she who slays demons), Bhairavi (the terrible one) and Sarhharini (she who destroys). Mahadevi's destructive features are further described in a hymn called Aryastava, which refers to her as Kalaratri (night of death) and Nistha (she who is death).

According to Shakta traditions, Devi is the ultimate goddess and the complete physical embodiment of Adi Parashakti. Brahma, Vishnu and Shiva of this brahman are her subordinates and cannot function without her power. Thus, she is considered the supreme goddess and primary deity in Shaktism as she is the closest representation of Adi Parashakti. Whatever deity one worships, whether it is Maha Kali, Maha Saraswati, Maha Lakshmi or even Mata Vaishno Devi, they are ultimately, worshiping Adi Parashakti.

All human beings contain attributes of the three abovementioned gunas, which the Tridevi represents, and the actions of the goddesses are determined by the guna that is predominant in their nature. But, in order to lead a meaningful life, a proper balance among these three is necessary. The holy cave is charged with energy that helps create this vital but rare balance in a person. This is what makes the holy shrine of Mata Vaishno Devi Ji unique in the entire world, and this is the reason why so many pilgrims come here every day.

Vaishno Devi Temple

TWO

# The Cult of Shakti

The Cult of Shakti, or Shaktism, as it is also known, is a school of thought in Hinduism wherein reality is considered to exist in the form of a woman, and Shakti (Mahadevi) is regarded as the supreme godhead. It includes many goddesses, all considered aspects of the same supreme goddess, much in the same way as Vaishno Devi, who is considered to be combined energies of three primary goddesses. Shaktism has different subtraditions, ranging from those focussed on Durga, to those centred around gracious Parvati, to that of the fierce Kali. These different subtraditions are not divergent or separate, but flow into one another, enhancing each other and making Shaktism a compound and complex philosophical school.

Shaktism is known for its various subtraditions of Tantras, as well as a galaxy of goddesses with respective systems. The most common aspects of Devi found in Shaktism include Durga, Kali, Saraswati, Lakshmi, Parvati and Tripurasundari. The goddess-focussed tradition is very popular in eastern India, particularly in West Bengal, Odisha, Bihar, Jharkhand, Tripura and Assam—regions that celebrate festivals such as the Durga Puja.

Shaktism also emphasizes that intense love of the deity is more important than simple obedience, thus showing the influence of Vaishnava ideas, where a passionate, devoted relationship is also the ideal relationship. These older ideas still influence modern Shaktism. Similarly, Shaktism's ideas have also influenced Vaishnavism and Shaivism traditions. In Shaktism, the goddess is considered to be the shakti/energy of Vishnu and Shiva, and is revered prominently.

## History

The history of the cult of Shakti is as old, if not older, than Hinduism. While the origins are not clear, it has been reported that the worship of Shakti or Mahadevi has been going on in the subcontinent for the last 8,000 years.

Thus, the cult of Shakti is, in some ways, the original religion of India and was primarily practised by the tribals inhabiting the subcontinent prior to the arrival of farmers. Once the first farmers in India arrived in Mehrgarh, which was one of the earliest sites of occupation of the Indus Valley Civilization, this school of thought and tradition was adopted by them. It was adopted by subsequent settlements in the following centuries. There is evidence of worship of the feminine and the early beginnings of a cult of Shakti present throughout the territory covered by the Indus Valley Civilization. The Indus Valley period is also the first time that the presence of other sacred symbols, such as the *yoni*, started and spread throughout the subcontinent.

The Indus Valley Civilization

After the fall of the Indus Valley Civilization, the worship of Devi and Shakti continued even with the arrival of the Vedic Age. The Vedic Age brought about a new pantheon of gods, and in this pantheon, the devis belonging to the Cult of Shakti found their place. This was the period when Shaktism became codified, as the Vedic Age also brought with it writing and texts that were written to formulate rituals and ceremonies. The most important of the female deities mentioned in the Vedas is Ushas. A number of hymns in the Vedas are dedicated exclusively to her. The three Divine Mothers mentioned in the Rig Veda who birthed the Vedic gods are Aditi, Prithvi and Saraswati. Prithvi continued to exist in later Hinduism as Bhudevi (goddess of the earth).

Goddess Ushas

Aditi: The Goddess of Infinity

The historically recurring theme of the Devi being all-encompassing arises for the first time in such declarations as this one in the first book of the Rig Veda: 'Aditi is the sky, Aditi is the air, Aditi is all gods ... Aditi is the mother, the father and the son. Aditi is whatever shall be born.'

Also significant is the appearance of two of Hinduism's most widely known and beloved goddesses in the famous hymn from the Rig Veda: Vac, identified with the present-day Saraswati; and Shri, better known today as Lakshmi. In the hymn, still recited by thousands of Hindus each day, the goddess unambiguously declares:

> I am the Sovereign Queen; the treasury of all treasures; the chief of all objects of worship;

> whose all-pervading Self manifests all gods and goddesses; whose birthplace is in the midst of the causal waters; who in breathing forth gives birth to all created worlds, and yet extends beyond them, so vast am I in greatness. (Mandala X)

The great Kena Upanishad (c. 750–500 BCE) tells an early tale in which the Devi appears as shakti, or essential power, of the supreme brahman. It begins with the Vedic trinity of Agni, Vayu and Indra boasting and posturing in the flush of a recent victory over a demon hoard, until they suddenly find themselves bereft of divine power in the presence of a mysterious *yaksha* or forest spirit. When Indra tries to approach and question the yaksha, it disappears, replaced by the Devi in the form of a well-adorned yakshini:

> It was Uma, the daughter of Himavat. Indra said to her, 'Who was that yaksha?' She replied, 'It is brahman. It is only through the victory of brahman that you have thus become great.' After that, Indra and the devas realized the Truth ... having known brahman through such direct experience. (Kena Upanishad III)

Therefore, Shakti is present throughout most of the foundational texts of Vedic Hinduism as well as in other literary creations of the late Vedic period. While there is no presence of a Shakti Devi in the Ramayana, she is mentioned prominently in the Mahabharata in the form of Durga, with her residence in the Vindhyas, reiterating that the cult of Shakti first existed among the tribal groups of India.

Vishnu and His Avatars

In time and with the rise of violence-prone and patriarchal societies, the female deities have been replaced by male deities across the world. But in India, this did not change much. Male gods in India have always existed alongside female deities, and even though they have acquired more prominence lately, our female goddesses have not been ignored as a result of this. They continue to be honoured and respected on their own merit and as graceful consorts of male deities—Parvati as Shiva's consort, Lakshmi as Vishnu's and Saraswati as Brahma's. Additionally, powerful goddesses like Durga and Kali have largely kept their independent status; they are revered and popular even today. In India, there is hardly a town or a village that does not have a shrine dedicated to the Mata or the Devi. Within the school of Indian spirituality, the feminine has always occupied a prominent position, and the Mother Goddess is usually considered the Eternal Mother, who is filled with wisdom, beauty, compassion, perfection and strength. The following lyrics from Saktisangama Tantra show the amount of respect accorded to a woman in Hinduism:

> Woman is the creator of the Universe,
> The Universe is her form;
> Woman is the foundation of the world,
> She is the true form of the body.
> Whatever form she takes,
> Whether the form of a man or a woman,
> Is the superior form.
> In woman is the form of all things,
> Of all that lives and moves in the world.
> There is no jewel rarer than woman,

No condition superior to that of a woman.
There is not, nor has been, nor will be
Any destiny to equal that of a woman;
There is no kingdom, no wealth,
To be compared with a woman;
There is not, nor has been, nor will be
Any holy place like unto a woman.
There is no prayer to equal a woman.
There is not, nor has been, nor will be
Any yoga to compare with a woman,
No mystical formula nor asceticism
To match a woman.
There are not, nor have been, nor will be
Any riches more valuable than woman.

There are many reasons behind why the Mother Goddess continues to remain so venerated and a significant part and pillar of Hinduism. Most of the shrines that have come into being to honour the Mother Goddess have existed through centuries. Therefore, a real and material presence, combined with the continued popularity of the shrines, has ensured that the Mother Goddess has not lost her significance, on top of which is the fact that Shaktism is, in essence, a feminine version of Vedanta, which is the core philosophy of Hinduism itself.

## Shaktism and Bhakti

Some of the foremost texts in Hinduism written after the Vedic Period are the Puranas. The Puranas, being written late in antiquity during the Gupta Period, afford us a glimpse into understanding Hinduism and its pantheon of gods and goddesses from a modern stand point, as opposed to the Vedas, which were mostly written in an archaic tongue.

Of the Puranas, the most important one when it comes to Shaktism is the Markandeya Purana. The most significant text of Shaktism is the Devi Mahatmya (also known as the Durga Saptashati, Chandi or Chandi-Path), which has been extracted from the Markandeya Purana. Composed some 1,600 years ago, the text weaves together diverse threads of ancient myths and creates a dazzling narrative that remains even today the central text of Shaktism. Here, for the first time, the various mythological and theological elements relating to devis were brought together and given a coherent and consistent form.

As the earliest Hindu scripture of divine femininity and goddess worship, the Devi Mahatmya also marks the birth of 'independent Shaktism', that is, the cult of the feminine as a distinct entity within Hinduism.

After the Devi Mahatmya, there are other texts that also talk in detail about Shakti and Shaktism, such as the Shakta Upanishad, which was written around the same time as the Devi Mahatmya. The Brahmanda Purana is also an important text when it comes to Shaktism.

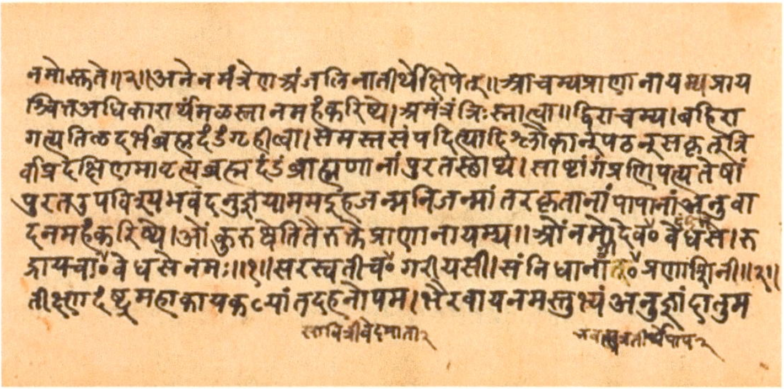

The Puranas

Similarly, the Lalita Sahasranama is among the earlier texts important in Shaktism before the arrival of the Bhakti Movement. It is part of the Brahmanda Purana, but its specific origins and authorship are lost in history. Based on textual evidence, it is believed to have been composed in South India not earlier than the ninth century CE or later than the eleventh century CE. The text is closely associated with another section of the Brahmanda Purana titled Lalitopakhyana (The Great Narrative of Lalita), which worships the deeds of the goddess in her form as Lalita-Tripurasundari, in particular her slaying of the demon Bhandasura.

With the advent of the Bhakti Movement, Shaktism was further developed in terms of traditions and rituals.

This was the period when the most amount of literature regarding the worship and glory of Shakti were written as well as when the discovery of the Shakti Peethas and pilgrimages happened. In most schools of Shaktism, the Tantras are central scriptures. The Tantras devised two main *margas* (paths of sadhana) to reach the same goal.

Around 800 CE, Adi Shankara, the legendary sage and preceptor of the Advaita Vedanta system, implicitly recognized Shakta philosophy and Tantric liturgy as part of mainstream Hinduism in his powerful and still hugely popular hymn known as 'Saundaryalahari' (Waves of Beauty). Shankara, while not a Shakta in the sectarian sense, had a soft corner for Shakta religion, perhaps due to its popularity among the masses. Another important Shakta text often attributed to Shankara is the Mahishasura Mardini Stotra, a 21-verse hymn derived from the Devi Mahatmya that constitutes one of the greatest works ever addressed to the supreme feminine power.

By the thirteenth century, the Tantras assimilated a very large number of cults of various origins and assumed a completely Shakta character. From the fourteenth century, the Shakta–Tantric beliefs became woven into the fabric of all the religious practices in India, with their spirit and substance infusing regional as well as Sanskrit literature.

Adi Shankara and His Disciples

At their roots, the Shakti of Mother Goddess and the Brahma of Vedanta are one and the same. In other words, the cult of Shakti is merely Vedanta in its female avatar. As the great thinker Ramakrishna Parmahansa has said:

> What is milk like? Oh, you say, it is something white. You cannot think of the milk without the whiteness, and again, you cannot think of the whiteness without the milk. Thus one cannot think of Brahman without Sakti, or of Sakti without Brahman. One cannot think of the Absolute

> without the Relative, or of the Relative without the Absolute.*

Both Vedanta and Shakti have the same fundamental philosophy. It is about looking inwards and filling oneself with spiritual energy. This allows us to stay aware of our true nature and to embrace the god within us. The main idea here is to remember that it does not matter if the divinity is revered as male or female; the focus needs to be on the meditation and concentration that makes us peaceful, awakens our spiritual self and helps others do so too.

## Shakti Peethas and Their Origins

The Shakti Peethas are shrines and pilgrimage destinations of high importance in Shaktism. The shrines are dedicated to the many forms and incarnations of Mahadevi. Various Puranas, such as Srimad Devi Bhagavatam, state the existence of varying numbers of 52, 64 and 108 Shakti Peethas, of which 18 are named as Astadasha Maha in medieval Hindu texts. Most of the Shakti Peethas are in India, but there are seven in Bangladesh, three in Pakistan, three in Nepal and one each in Tibet and Sri Lanka.

The origin of the Shakti Peethas is detailed in one

*'Attraction towards Sai Baba's clothes', *Sai Baba of Shirdi—A Blog*, 19 December 2020, https://tinyurl.com/5eezbc3y. Accessed on 21 August 2023.

of the most important events in Hinduism called the Daksha Yajna. The tale is mainly told in the Vayu Purana. It is also mentioned in the Kasi Kanda of the Skanda Purana, the Kurma Purana, the Harivamsa Purana and the Padma Purana. The Linga Purana, the Shiva Purana and the Matsya Purana also detail the incident. Variations of the legend may be observed in later Puranas.

Daksha was one of the Prajapatis, a son of Brahma. He was considered to be among Brahma's foremost creations. He married Manu's daughter Prasuti. Sati (also known as Uma) was his youngest daughter and also his favourite.

Sati was deeply in love with Shiva and wished to become his wife. Her worship of and devotion towards Shiva strengthened her immense desire to wed him. However, Daksha did not like his daughter's yearning for Shiva, mainly because he was a Prajapati and the son of the god Brahma, and Sati was a royal princess. They were wealthy nobility, and their royal lifestyle was entirely different from that of the laidback and informal Shiva. As a king, Daksha wanted to increase his influence and power by making marriage alliances with powerful kingdoms, and influential sages and deities.

Shiva, on the other hand, led a very modest life. He lived among the downtrodden, wore tiger skin, smeared ash on his body, had thick locks of matted hair and was an impartial god. His abode was Mount Kailash in the Himalayas. He embraced all kinds of living beings and did not make any distinction between good and bad souls. The Bhutaganas, his followers, consisted of all kinds of ghosts, demons, ghouls and goblins. He wandered through gardens and graveyards alike. As a consequence, Daksha disliked Shiva as his daughter's companion. However, unlike Daksha, Sati loved Shiva. She won Shiva as her husband by performing severe *tapas* (austerities). Despite Daksha's disapproval, she married Shiva.

Brahma

Shiva and Sati

Once, Brahma conducted a huge *yajna* (ritual sacrifice), where all the Prajapatis, deities and kings of the world were invited. Shiva and Sati were also called on to participate in the yajna. All of them arrived and sat in their assigned ceremonial places. Daksha came last. When he arrived, everyone in the yajna, with the exception of Brahma and Shiva, stood up, showing their reverence for him. Brahma, being Daksha's father, did not rise. Shiva, being Daksha's son-in-law, and also due to the fact that he was superior in stature to Daksha, remained seated. Daksha misunderstood Shiva's gesture and considered this act an insult. Daksha vowed to take revenge for the insult in the same manner.

Daksha's grudge towards Shiva grew after Brahma's yajna. With the prime motive of insulting Shiva, Daksha initiated a great yajna, similar to that of Brahma. The Bhagavata Purana mentions its name as Brihaspatistava. The yajna was to be presided over by Sage Bhrigu. He invited all the deities, Prajapatis and kings to attend the yajna, and intentionally avoided inviting Shiva and Sati. Despite being invited, Brahma and Vishnu declined to attend the yajna in the Skanda Purana.

The Kurma Purana discusses the dialogues between Sage Dadhichi and Daksha. After the sacrifice and hymns were offered to the 12 Aditya deities, Dadhichi noticed that there was no *havvis* (sacrificial portion) allotted to Shiva and his wife, and no Vedic hymns were used in the yajna addressing Shiva. He warned Daksha that he was not to alter the Vedas for personal reasons; the priests and sages supported this. Daksha replied to Dadhichi that he would not do so, and insulted Shiva through this very act. Dadhichi left the yajna because of this argument.

Sati came to know about the grand yajna organized by her father and asked Shiva to attend it. Shiva refused her request, saying that it was inappropriate to attend a function without being invited. He reminded her that they had not being invited intentionally. Sati was of the notion that there was no need for them to have received an invitation in order to attend as she was

Daksha's favourite daughter and no formality existed between them. She constantly pleaded with Shiva to let her attend the yajna and turned a deaf ear to her husband's reasoning. Relenting, Shiva allowed Sati to go to her parents' home with his followers, including Nandi, but refused to accompany her.

Upon arriving, Sati tried to meet her parents and sisters. Daksha was arrogant and avoided interacting with Sati. He repeatedly snubbed her in front of all the dignitaries but Sati maintained her composure. Irritated by Sati's persistence in trying to meet him, Daksha reacted vehemently and insulted her in front of all the other guests at the yajna to which she had not been invited. He called Shiva an atheist and a cremation-ground dweller. As planned, he took advantage of the situation and continued shouting repugnant words against Shiva. Sati felt deep remorse for not listening to her beloved husband. Daksha's disdain towards her, and especially her husband Shiva, in front of all the guests, grew by the moment. The humiliation of her and her beloved eventually became too much for her to bear.

She cursed Daksha for acting so atrociously toward her and Shiva and reminded him that his haughty behaviour had blinded his intellect. She cursed him and warned that the wrath of Shiva would destroy him and his kingdom. Unable to bear further humiliation, Sati took her own life by jumping into the sacrificial fire. Other versions of the legend state that Sati lost all control over her anger, took the form of Adi Shakti or Durga and cursed Daksha to fall to ruin. She immolated her body using her own energy and returned to the Sarvaloka. The onlookers tried to save her, but it was too late. They were only able to retrieve the half-burnt body of Sati.

Nandi and the accompanying Bhutaganas left the yajna after the incident. Nandi cursed the participants and Bhrigu reacted by cursing the Bhutaganas back.

Shiva was deeply pained upon hearing of his wife's death. His grief grew into a terrible anger when he realized how Daksha's actions had contributed to his own daughter's demise. Shiva's rage became so intense that he plucked a lock of hair from his head and smashed it on the ground, breaking it into two with his leg. Two armed, fearsome beings, Virabhadra and Bhadrakali (Rudrakali), emerged. Shiva ordered them to kill Daksha and destroy the yajna.

Lord Virabhadra

Bhadrakali

The ferocious Virabhadra and Bhadrakali, along with the Bhutaganas, reached the site of the yajna. At this, the invitees renounced the yajna and started running away from the violence. Sage Bhrigu created an army with his divine powers to resist Shiva's attack and protect the yajna, but it was demolished and the premises were ravaged. All those who participated, even the other Prajapatis and the deities, were beaten and even slaughtered mercilessly. The Vayu Purana mentions the attack of Bhutaganas: the nose of some goddesses were cut; Yama's staff bone was broken; Mitra's eyes were pulled out; Indra was trampled by Virabhadra and the Bhutaganas; Pushan's teeth were knocked out; Chandra was beaten heavily; all of the Prajapatis were injured; Vahini's hands were chopped off; and Bhrigu's beard was cut off.

There are three differing accounts of the conclusion of this conflict, one of which ends with Daksha's decapitation and two of which lead to an intervention by Parabrahman or Vishnu.

The Linga Purana and the Bhagavata Purana mention the decapitation of Daksha. He was caught and decapitated, and the attack stopped once the Bhutaganas started plucking out Bhrigu's white beard as a victory souvenir.

The Vayu Purana states that Yajneshwara, the personification of yajna, took the form of an antelope and jumped towards the sky. Virabhadra captured and decapitated it. Daksha begged the Parabrahman (the ultimate reality in Hinduism) for mercy, who rose from the yajna fire and forgave Daksha. The Parabhraman informed Daksha that Shiva was, in fact, a manifestation of itself. Daksha then became a great devotee of Shiva.

The Harivamsha Purana and the Kurma Purana describe a conflict between Vishnu and Shiva/ Virabhadra. In the Kurma Purana, Vishnu, riding upon Garuda, engaged in combat with Virabhadra, employing his Sudarshana Chakra. Virabhadra was able to fend off the attacks of the deity, and Brahma finally intervened to put an end to the violence by brokering a peace between Shiva and Daksha. In the Harivamsha Purana, Vishnu caught a hold of Shiva's throat, rendering it blue. Nandi struck Vishnu's head with the divine weapon Pinaka, which did not harm the preserver. When placated, Vishnu offered a portion of the sacrificial offerings to Shiva, restoring peace between the parties.

According to the Bhagavata Purana, since the obstruction of the yajna creates havoc upon nature and puts the world out of balance, Brahma and Vishnu went to the grief-stricken Shiva. They comforted and sympathized with him. They requested him to come to the yajna's location, pacify the Bhutaganas and allow the yajna to be completed. Shiva agreed. He found the burnt body of Sati and permitted the continuation of the yajna. Daksha was absolved by Shiva, and the head of a ram was fixed on the decapitated body of Daksha, restoring his life. The yajna was completed successfully.

In Shakta Puranas, such as the Devi Bhagavata Purana and the Kalika Purana, Shiva was distressed and could not part from his beloved wife. He took her corpse and wandered around the universe. To reduce Shiva's grief, Vishnu cut Sati's corpse according to the Vaishnava Puranas. The parts fell in the places Shiva wandered to. The Shaiva Puranas say that her body disintegrated on its own, and the parts fell while Shiva was carrying Sati's corpse to various places. These places commemorated each fallen body part and came to be known as the Shakti Peethas.

Shiva went into isolation and wandered all around the world until Sati reincarnated as Parvati, the daughter of the King Himavana. Like Sati, Parvati performed severe austerities, gave away all her royal privileges and went into the forest. Shiva eventually realized Parvati is Sati herself; he tested her affection and devotion in disguise. Later, he wed Parvati.

Table 1 lists 51 of the commonly accepted Shakti Peethas. The column of ' Shakti' in the table refers to the female incarnation of Mahadevi that is worshipped at that particular Shakti Peetha. For example, the Shakti in Katra is Vaishno Devi/Vaishnavi. Similarly, the column of 'Bhairava' refers to the identity of the male consort that the female incarnation is associated with. For instance, in the case of Vaishno Devi, it is Rama/Vishnu.

## Table 1:
## List of Commonly Accepted 51 Shakti Peethas

| S. No. | Place | State, Country | Body Part/ Ornament | Shakti | Bhairava |
|---|---|---|---|---|---|
| 1 | Amarnath: From Srinagar through Pahalgam, 94 km by bus; from Chandanwari, 16 km walking | Jammu & Kashmir, India | Throat | Mahamaya | Trisandhyeshwar |
| 2 | Attahas Village of Dakshindihi in the district of Bardhaman, near the Katwa Railway Station | West Bengal, India | Lips | Phullara | Vishvesh |
| 3 | Bahula, on the bank of the Ajay River in Ketugram, 8 km from Katwa, Burdwan | West Bengal, India | Left arm | Bahula | Bhiruk |

| S. No. | Place | State, Country | Body Part/ Ornament | Shakti | Bhairava |
|---|---|---|---|---|---|
| 4 | Bakreshwar, on the bank of the Paaphara River, 24 km from Siuri Town, Birbhum District; 7 km from Dubrajpur Railway Station | West Bengal, India | Portion between the eyebrows | Mahishmardini | Vakranath |
| 5 | Bhairavparvat in Bhairav Hills on the banks of the Shipra River in the city of Ujjaini | Madhya Pradesh, India | Elbow | Avanti | Lambkarna |
| 6 | Bhabanipur union in Karatoyatat, 28 km from interior Sherpur upazila, Ratnapore District | Bangladesh | Left anklet (ornament) | Arpana | Vaman |

| S. No. | Place | State, Country | Body Part/ Ornament | Shakti | Bhairava |
|---|---|---|---|---|---|
| 7 | Chhinnamastika Shakti Peeth at Chintpurni, in Una District | Himachal Pradesh, India | Feet | Chhinnamastika | Rudra Mahadev |
| 8 | Gandaki, Pokhara, about 125 km on the bank of Gandaki River, where Muktinath temple is situated | Nepal | Temple | Gandaki Chandi | Chakrapani |
| 9 | Goddess Bhadrakaali on the bank of Godavari in Nashik | Maharashtra, India | Chin (2 parts) | Bhramari | Vikritaksh |
| 10 | Hinglaj (or Hingula), southern Baluchistan, a few hours northeast of Gawadar and about 125 km towards northwest from Karachi | Pakistan | Bramharandhra (Part of the head) | Kottari | Bhimlochan |

| S. No. | Place | State, Country | Body Part/ Ornament | Shakti | Bhairava |
|---|---|---|---|---|---|
| 11 | Jayanti at Nartiang village in the Jaintia Hills District. This Shakti Peetha is locally known as the Nartiang Durga Temple | Meghalaya, India | Left thigh | Jayanti | Kramadishwar |
| 12 | Jessoreswari, situated at Ishwaripur, Shyamnagar, district Satkhira. The temple complex was built by Maharaja Pratapaditya, the capital of whose kingdom was Ishwaripur. | Bangladesh | Palms of hands and soles of the feet | Jashoreshwari | Chanda |

| S. No. | Place | State, Country | Body Part/ Ornament | Shakti | Bhairava |
|---|---|---|---|---|---|
| 13 | Jwalaji, Kangra, Pathankot to at Jwalamukhi Road Station and then 20 km ahead | Himachal Pradesh, India | Tongue | Siddhida (Ambika) | Unmatta Bhairav |
| 14 | Kalipeeth, Kalighat, Kolkata | West Bengal, India | Right toes | Kalika | Nakuleshwar |
| 15 | Kalmadhav, on the bank of Shon River in a cave over the hills near Amarkantak | Madhya Pradesh, India | Left buttock | Kali | Asitang |
| 16 | Kamgiri, Kamakhya, in the Neelachal Hills near Guwahati | Assam, India | Genitals | Kamakhya | Umanand |

| S. No. | Place | State, Country | Body Part/ Ornament | Shakti | Bhairava |
|---|---|---|---|---|---|
| 17 | Kankalitala, on the banks of Kopai River, 10 km northeast of Bolpur station in Birbhum District | West Bengal, India | Bone | Devgarbha | Ruru |
| 18 | Kanyashram of Balaambika, Bhagavathy temple in Kanyakumari, the southernmost tip of mainland India, Tamil Nadu (also thought to be situated in Yunnan province, China) | Tamil Nadu, India | Back | Sarvani | Nimish |
| 19 | Karnat, Brajeshwari Devi, Kangra | Himachal Pradesh, India | Both ears | Jayadurga | Abhiru |

| S. No. | Place | State, Country | Body Part/ Ornament | Shakti | Bhairava |
|---|---|---|---|---|---|
| 20 | Kireet at Kireetkona village, 3 km from Lalbag Court Road station, Murshidabad District | West Bengal, India | Crown | Vimla | Sanwart |
| 21 | Locally known as Anandamayee Temple, Ratnavali, on the banks of Ratnakar River at Khanakul-Krishnanagar, Hooghly District | West Bengal, India | Right shoulder | Kumari | Shiva |
| 22 | Locally known as Bhramari Devi, Jalpaiguri, near Boda on the banks of Teesta River | West Bengal, India | Left leg | Bhraamari | Ambar |

| S. No. | Place | State, Country | Body Part/ Ornament | Shakti | Bhairava |
|---|---|---|---|---|---|
| 23 | Manas in Tibet, at the foot of Mount Kailash, Lake Mansarovar | Tibet | Right hand | Dakshayani | Amar |
| 24 | Manibandh, Gayatri Hills, near Pushkar, 11 km northwest of Ajmer | Rajasthan, India | Two bracelets | Gayatri | Sarvanand |
| 25 | Mithila, near Janakpur railway station, on the border of India and Nepal | Nepal | Left shoulder | Uma | Mahodar |
| 26 | Nainativu (Manipallavam), Northern Province, Sri Lanka, 36 km from the ancient capital of the Jaffna Kingdom, Nallur | Sri Lanka | Silambu (Anklets) | Indrakshi (Nagapooshani/ Bhuvaneswari) | Rakshaseshwar (Nayanair) |

| S. No. | Place | State, Country | Body Part/ Ornament | Shakti | Bhairava |
|---|---|---|---|---|---|
| 27 | Guhyeshwari Temple | Nepal | Both knees | Mahashira | Kapali |
| 28 | On Chandranath Hill, near Sitakunda station, Chittagong District, Bangladesh | Bangladesh | Right arm | Bhawani | Chandrashekhar |
| 29 | Panchsagar, near Lohaghat, Champawat District, Uttarakhand, nearly 100 km from nearest railway station, Tanakpur | Uttarakhand, India | Lower teeth | Varahi | Maharudra |
| 30 | Prabhas, 4 km from Veraval station, near Somnath temple, Junagadh District | Gujarat, India | Stomach | Chandrabhaga | Vakratund |

| S. No. | Place | State, Country | Body Part/ Ornament | Shakti | Bhairava |
|---|---|---|---|---|---|
| 31 | Prayag, near Sangam, Prayagraj | Uttar Pradesh, India | Finger | Lalita | Bhava |
| 32 | Kurukshetra | Haryana, India | Ankle bone | Savitri/Bhadrakali | Sthanu |
| 33 | Ramgiri, Chitrakuta, on the Jhansi–Manikpur railway line | Uttar Pradesh, India | Right breast | Shivani | Chanda |
| 34 | Sainthia, locally known as Nandikeshwari temple, 1.5 km from the railway station under a banyan tree within a boundary wall, Birbhum District | West Bengal, India | Necklace | Nandini | Nandikeshwar |

| S. No. | Place | State, Country | Body Part/ Ornament | Shakti | Bhairava |
|---|---|---|---|---|---|
| 35 | Sarvashail or Godavaritir, Kotilingeswar temple, on the banks of Godavari River near Rajamundry | Andhra Pradesh, India | Cheeks | Rakini or Vishweshwari | Vatsnabh or Dandpani |
| 36 | Naina Devi, Nainital | Uttarakhand, India | Eyes | Mahishmardini | Krodhish |
| 37 | Shondesh, at the source point of Narmada River, Amarkantak | Madhya Pradesh, India | Right buttock | Narmada | Bhadrasen |
| 38 | Shri Parvat, near Ladakh (also thought to be situated in Srisailam, Shriparvat Hills, Kurnool District) | Andhra Pradesh, India | Right anklet | Shrisundari | Sundaranand |

| S. No. | Place | State, Country | Body Part/ Ornament | Shakti | Bhairava |
|---|---|---|---|---|---|
| 39 | Shri Shail, Joinpur village, Dakshin Surma, near Gotatikar, 3 km northeast of Sylhet town | Bangladesh | Neck | Maha Lakshmi | Sambaranand |
| 40 | Shuchi, Shiva temple, Suchindrum, 11 km on Kanyakumari–Thiruvananthapuram road | Tamil Nadu, India | Upper teeth | Narayani | Sanhar |
| 41 | Sugandha, Shikarpur, Gournadi, about 20 km from Barisal town, Bangladesh, on the banks of Sonda River | Bangladesh | Nose | Sugandha | Trayambak |

| S. No. | Place | State, Country | Body Part/ Ornament | Shakti | Bhairava |
|---|---|---|---|---|---|
| 42 | Tripura Sundari temple near Radhakishorepur village, a little distance away from Udaipur town | Tripura, India | Right leg | Tripura Sundari | Tripuresh |
| 43 | Ujaani, 16 km from Guskara station under Burdwan district | West Bengal, India | Right wrist | Mangal Chandika | Kapilambar |
| 44 | Varanasi, Manikarnika Ghat, on the banks of the Ganges at Kashi | Uttar Pradesh, India | Earring | Vishalakshi and Manikarni | Kalbhairav |
| 45 | Vibhash, Tamluk, Purba Medinipur District | West Bengal, India | Left ankle | Kapalini (Bhimarupa) | Sarvanand |
| 46 | Virat, near Bharatpur | Rajasthan, India | Left toes | Ambika | Amriteshwar |

| S. No. | Place | State, Country | Body Part/ Ornament | Shakti | Bhairava |
|---|---|---|---|---|---|
| 47 | Vrindavan, near the new bus stand on Bhuteshwar road within Bhuteshwar Mahadev Temple, Katyayanipeeth | Uttar Pradesh, India | Ringlets of hair | Uma | Bhutesh |
| 48 | Devi Talab Mandir, Jalandhar | Punjab, India | Left breast | Tripurmalini | Bhutesh |
| 49 | Baidyanath Dham | Jharkhand, India | Heart | Jaya Durga | Baidyanath |
| 50 | Bhairabkund Shiva Temple | Bhutan | | | |
| 51 | Jogadya, at Kshirgam | West Bengal | Big toe | Jogadya | Ksheer Kantak |

## The Discovery of Vaishno Devi

Among the many legends associated with the shrine of Mata Vaishno Devi is that of the previously discussed encounter between Lord Rama and Vaishnavi during the period of his exile when he directed the goddess towards the holy cave situated in Trikoot Parbat. There are other legends too, like that of the Pandavas who are said to have visited the holy abode and are also believed to have built a temple here. Prahalad, the legendary son of the atheist king Hirankashayap, is also believed to have undertaken a pilgrimage to the holy shrine. However, the most popular and well-known legend is that of Sridhar Brahmin, who used to live in village called Hansali, situated at the foot of Trikoot Parbat, adjacent to modern-day Katra.

Sridhar was a staunch devotee of Shakti. Even though he was a very poor man, with the inspiration and assurance from Goddess Vaishanavi, who appeared one day in his dream in *kanayaroop*, Sridhar undertook organizing a grand bhandara. An auspicious date for the bhandara was selected, and he invited all the people living in nearby villages. Thereafter, he went from door to door requesting his neighbours and acquaintances to give him raw provisions, which could be cooked and served to the guests on the day of the bhandara. Though a few of them obliged, many others turned down his request. They, in fact, taunted him for having the audacity to hold a bhandara without having the wherewithal for it. As the day of bhandara drew closer, Sridhar's worries about feeding the guests invited for the bhandara also increased.

On the night preceding the day of the bhandara, Sridhar could not sleep a wink. He had spent the entire night grappling with the problem of how to feed his guests with the limited provisions and accommodate them in the inadequate space that he had. When he was unable to come up with a satisfactory solution to his problems till morning, he resigned himself to fate and got up to face the day. He sat down for puja outside his hut. By midday, his guests started arriving. Finding him deeply involved in the puja, they began to make themselves comfortable wherever they could find place. Strangely enough, a very large number of guests were able to comfortably have their space inside Sridhar's small hut with a lot of space left unutilized. When the puja was over, Sridhar looked around and saw the huge number of guests who had arrived. While he was wondering how to tell his guests that he would not be able feed them, he saw Vaishnavi coming out of his hut. With her grace, all guests were offered food of their choice, and the bhandara turned out to be very successful.

After the bhandara, Sridhar was curious to get to the bottom of the mystery about Vaishanavi. He wanted to ask young Vaishnavi for an explanation for the mysterious developments of the day. He called out to her, but Vaishanavi was not there to reply. He called out again and again but with the same result. Vaishnavi was nowhere to be seen. A feeling of emptiness engulfed Sridhar. Then, one day, he had a dream of the same girl; she told him that she was Vaishno Devi. The goddess showed him the vision of her cave and blessed him with the boon of four sons. Sridhar, happy once again, set out in search of the cave, and after finding it, he decided to spend rest of his life in worship of the deity. Soon, the fame of the holy cave spread, and devotees began to flock it to pay homage to the mighty Goddess.

Aarti at the Bhawan

THREE

# The Myths of Shakti

There are several stories of Mahadevi or Shakti that have helped cement her status as one of the most prominent goddess in Hinduism and are the reason behind her everlasting popularity and devotion. Some stories have been heard, such as the destruction of the demon Mahishasura. Others are less well known but are often told among the Devi's faithful following. Devotees might even end up hearing one or more of them on their pilgrimage to Trikuta. These stories and episodes are what keep the *bhakti* towards Mahadevi alive, and are a necessary part of understanding and following Shaktism and the Call of the Mata.

## The Story of Madhu and Kaithab

At the beginning of time, there was only the primeval ocean all around. Vishnu lay on Sheshnag in deep slumber under the influence of Yoga Nidra. While Vishnu slept, a lotus stalk grew out of his navel. At the upper end of the stalk was a lotus flower. Brahma was born in the lotus flower and was in deep meditation at the time of his birth. As Brahma lay in deep meditation, reciting the Vedas, ear wax flowed out of both ears of Vishnu.

Two asuras known as Madhu and Kaitabh were born out of the ear wax. These asuras performed great penance for thousands of years. The Devi was pleased with their devotion. She appeared before them and granted them the boon that death would come to them only when they desired it. Being conscious of their immense strength, both asuras became arrogant. They attacked Brahma and stole the four Vedas from him. Brahma, though furious, was helpless in the face of the might of the asuras. Hence, he rushed to Vishnu in great consternation to seek his protection.

Vishnu, however, was in deep sleep under the influence of Yoga Nidra and did not wake up, inspite of Brahma's best efforts. When Brahma realized that he could not wake up Vishnu, he then beseeched and praised Yoga Nidra to help him awaken Vishnu. Brahma's fervent prayers pleased Yoga Nidra. She took pity on Brahma's plight and left Vishnu's body. As soon as Yoga Nidra left his body, Vishnu woke up. Brahma told him about the murderous intent of Madhu and Kaitabh and entreated him to destroy them. Thus, Lord Vishnu engaged in a fierce and long battle with the two asuras, at the end of which he killed them. In the story of Madhu and Kaitabh, Goddess Durga has been portrayed as Yoga Nidra, whose powerful influence renders even Lord Vishnu helpless.

Vishnu Killing Madhu and Kaitabha

## The Story of Mahishasura

Mahishasura is a bovine asura in Hinduism. He is depicted in literature to be a deceitful demon who pursued his evil ways by shape-shifting. He was ultimately killed by Goddess Durga with her trishul, after which she gained the epithet Mahishasuramardini. The Navaratri festival celebrates this battle between Mahishasura and Durga, culminating in Vijaya Dasami, a celebration of her ultimate victory. This story depicts the 'triumph of good over evil'; carries profound symbolism in Hinduism, particularly Shaktism; and is both narrated as well as reenacted from the Devi Mahatmya at many South and Southeast Asian Hindu temples.

Mahishasura the demon was born as a union of Rambha, the great-grandson of Brahmarshi Kashyapa, and a she-buffalo (*mahishi*). Consequently, he was half-man and half-buffalo. The mighty demon was rendered more powerful as a result of a boon from God Agni, according to which he could be killed only by a woman. He managed to wreak havoc in heaven by chasing away all gods from there. All the gods then approached Lord Vishnu and Lord Shiva, who were aware that only a woman could kill Mahishasura. They decided to create a goddess out of the tejas of all the gods, and, so, a goddess was born, who contained in herself all that was mighty and powerful in each god. She was armed with a trident from Shiva, a chakra from Vishnu, a lion from the Himalayas and bows and arrows from Vayu. The goddess, full of combined power and anger of all the gods, was fierce to behold and her very sight scared the demons.

Durga Killing Mahishasura

Mahishasura, on the other hand, waged a valiant fight against her and assumed the form of a buffalo, a lion, a man carrying a sword, an elephant and, lastly, again a buffalo. The battle raged on for 10,000 years and, finally, the goddess was able to pin down Mahishasura and chop off his head. The gods, rid of the demon, showered the goddess with innumerable praises and prayed to her with reverence to appear every time they were in need of her. Granting the same to the gods, she disappeared, only to appear again when called upon with devotion.

## The Story of Vritrasura

As per the ancient literatures and as contained in the Gita and other religious books, there was once a Prajapati named Tvashta, who had a devout and pious son named Vishwarupa. Vishwarupa, blessed with three heads, was a sage, having immense spiritual strengths, which evoked a sense of insecurity and fear in the mind of Lord Indra, the king of the Inderlok (paradise), and, in a fit of rage, Indra killed the good sage. When Prajapati Tvashta came to know of the incident, he became furious and performed a yajna with the purpose of avenging the death of his dear son. From the holy fire, another son of Tvashta was born, whom he named as Vritrasura and whose sole aim in life was to avenge his brother's death by destroying Indra.

Vritrasura then meditated and undertook penance, the result of which was that he was granted a supreme boon. As per this boon, no weapon known till then could kill him, and he would not die of anything that was either wet or dry or any weapon made of wood or metal. The boon also ensured that his power would go on increasing during the battle. Upon being granted this boon, Vritrasura waged a battle against Indra, and his forces and managed to deliver a crushing defeat as a result of which Indra had to flee from the battle scene, leaving behind his elephant Airawat. Vritrasura then took over Inderlok, forcing Indra to flee to Lord Shiva for help. Shiva, along with Brahma, went to Lord Vishnu to seek his help. Vishnu advised them that they should first win the confidence of Vritrasura, befriend him and then kill him when he may not be on his guard. Vishnu also advised them that they should pray to Shakti so that through her *yogmaya*, she may render Vritrasura incapable of intelligent thought. Indra did as advised and was consequently blessed by Shakti.

After this, Indra managed to befriend Vritrasura, and once, when Vritrasura was asleep on a seashore, Indra collected sea foam, as it was neither wet nor dry, neither wood nor any metal and it certainly could not be categorized as a weapon. With the intention of using the sea foam as a weapon to kill Vritrasura, Indra summoned

Mahadevi to enter the foam. When the goddess entered the foam, Indra wrapped it around his Vajra (a deadly, fierce and favourite weapon of Lord Indra, made from the bones donated by Sage Dadhichi), and with it, he killed Vritrasura there and then. The devas, rid of the menace of Vritrasura, praised Shakti for keeping her promise of helping them in their hour of need.

Lord Indra Killing Vritrasura

## The Story of Indra's Penance Following the Slaying of Vritrasura

After Vritrasura had been killed, all the saints and sages felt guilty about their dubious deed of having killed a brahmin who had left for the forest for meditation and peace. When Tvashta, Vritrasur's father, heard that his son had been killed by Indra through nefarious designs, he cursed Indra that he, too, would have to suffer a similar fate. Whispers of Indra's act started to spread all over, and all his lustre began to fade. With each passing day, Indra started becoming more remorseful of his sin of killing a brahmin.

One day, he left his palace for Lake Mansarovar and immersed himself in the stem of a lotus so as to be found by none. He was so overwrought by his sinful conduct that, in his despair, he forgot the necessary duties he was supposed to perform. Indra's sudden disappearance caused a chaos among the devas as clouds stopped pouring, wind stopped blowing and the lands became infertile. The devas thought of placing someone in Indra's seat as his proxy to smoothly carry on with the celestial order till the time he could be located. All devas decided to place Sage Nahush on his throne. Although Nahush was a saintly person, as soon as he ascended to the office of Indra, his outlook towards life was completely transformed, and he started partaking in sensual pleasures.

One day, he demanded that Indra's wife Indrani should be called to please him. Indrani turned to Brihaspati, the guru of all devas, for help and reached his ashram. Brihaspati advised her to gain time by telling Nahush that she is willing to serve him but after knowing whether her husband is alive or not. Brihaspati also advised to pray to Vishnu. Lord Vishnu, on being pleased with her prayers, suggested that Indrani should worship the goddess and perform an Ashwamedha Yajan to seek her forgiveness for Indra's sin of killing a brahmin so as to accelerate the process of the restoration of Indra's power and the end of Nahush's era.

Indrani started praying to the goddess with vigour and devotion. The goddess was pleased and appeared before her to grant her the boon. Indrani requested for reunion with her husband, the restoration of his powers and her rescue from Nahush. The goddess granted her the boons desired. On locating Indra, Indrani apprised him of Nahush's dubious demands.

As a strategy to tackle the unacceptable demands of Nahush, Indrani went to him and told him that she was ready to please him provided he could locate Indra and if he came to her in a unique carriage, driven by the great sages themselves. By this time, the maya of the goddess overpowered Nahush. He ordered the sages to pull his chariot to make his way to Indrani. They were bemused but agreed to it. The chariot driven by the sages left for Brihaspati's ashram. The thought of possessing Indrani excited Nahush so much that he began to urge the sages to move faster by repeatedly saying '*sarp*'. 'Sarp' means to move faster in Sanskrit, but it also means 'snake'. This annoyed the sages, who had so far been patient and merely curious about what was happening.

Finally, when the anger of the saints could not be contained, they cursed Nahush to become a snake for a thousand years. This curse lasted till he met Yudhishthir, the Pandav, who released him from it. Brihaspati and the other devas then went to Lake Mansarovar and requested Indra to come out of his hiding place and retake his position as the king of Devloka.

## The Story of Shumbha and Nishumbha

As per the known stories derived from the Shrimad Devi Bhagwat Purana, Shumbha and Nishumbha were two asura brothers who managed to obtain a boon from Lord Brahma that they will not be killed by any male, whether human being, animal, bird, or any other creature, but by a woman only. They desired this boon thinking that they will live for ever as they did not know of a lady who was so powerful as to kill them both in a war. Thus empowered, these demons started disturbing the prayers of the saints, torturing them and asking them to worship the duo rather than any other deity. The devas, realizing that they could not defeat the two brothers, remembered the promise of the goddess to come to their aid. They, then, praised the deity by saying that she was omnipotent, resided in each and every emotion and sensation of all beings in this universe.

While the gods were thus engaged, Parvati happened to pass by and when the prayers of the gods fell into her ears, she was moved to pity. Thus, she created another goddess from her own being who came to be known as Kaushiki. After the emergence of the goddess, Parvati turned black, thus, becoming known as Kalika. The goddess, thus born, was supremely beautiful, and when Chanda and Munda, the disciples of the demon brothers Shumbha and Nishumbha, set eyes upon her, they reported of her beauty to their gurus at once. Upon hearing of her beauty, the two brothers sent a marriage proposal to the goddess. The goddess told them that she had taken a vow to marry the one who could vanquish her in battle and take her forcibly. Thus incited into a battle by the goddess, Shumbha and Nishumbha first sent a large army and their able generals to beat this beautiful lady, but after they were defeated, the brothers sent Chanda and Munda. They, too, were defeated by the goddess, who assumed the form of Maha Kali. Thus, the goddess is also called Chamunda—the one who beheaded the asuras Chanda and Munda.

As the battle became more and more fierce, seven more goddesses or Shaktis emerged from the bodies of seven devas to assist the Goddess in this battle. At that time, the all-powerful demon Raktabija was sent to the battlefield. He had been granted the strange boon that wherever his blood would fall on the ground, it would act as a *bija* or seed and another Raktabija would sprout from it. To slay him, the goddess asked Kali to lick the blood of Raktabija before it fell on the ground. The goddess, in the meantime, beheaded the demons. All the Shaktis then together killed Nishumbha and his army, leaving just Shumbha. When Shumbha realized that he was outnumbered, he taunted the goddess that she alone could not defeat him and needed the help of seven other goddesses to do so. The goddess got infuriated. She merged all Shaktis into herself and single-handedly killed Shumbha, thus freeing the world of evil.

*Yatris* on Their Way to the Bhawan

FOUR

# The Yatra

The pilgrimage to Vaishno Devi includes traversing Banganga, Charan Paduka and Adhkuwari before reaching the Bhawan. Along the pilgrimage path, devotees also have a chance to pay respects and seek blessings of other divine beings that have visited the Trikuta Hill as well as trace the deeds of Vaishno Devi.

While pilgrims can undertake the pilgrimage from anywhere they see fit, the major stops on the traditional pilgrimage route exist Katra onwards. The first stop on the traditional pilgrimage route is the Darshani Deodi (meaning entrance) or Darshani Darwaza. The Darshani Deodi, also known as the Vaishno Devi Bhawan Deodi, is a stunning gateway made of white marble.

The Darshani Darwaza

As one enters the Darshani Deodi, one is greeted by the sounds of devotional music and the chanting of hymns by devotees. The gate is also adorned with beautiful floral decorations and is lit up during special occasions and festivals, adding to its splendor.

The Darshani Deodi is also considered a place of great spiritual significance, as it is believed that the blessings of Goddess Vaishno Devi are showered upon those who enter the temple through this gate. Pilgrims visiting the temple often stand at the gate for a few moments to seek the goddess's blessings and guidance on their spiritual journey. It is also a symbol of devotion, faith and spiritual enlightenment. Millions of devotees flock to the temple every year to offer their prayers and seek the blessings of the goddess, making it one of the most revered and visited pilgrimage sites in India.

About a kilometre ahead from the Darshani Deodi lies Banganga. The name of this river comes from two terms, '*ban*' and 'Ganga'. 'Ban' means arrow and 'Ganga' refers to the sacred river Ganges. It is a revered holy stream flowing in that region. As discussed previously,

The Banganga River

it is believed that Mata Vaishno Devi, while on her way to the holy cave, created this water body with an arrow from her quiver; hence, it is called Banganga. It is also said that she took a dip in it and washed her hair there.

Thus, some people also prefer to call it Bal Ganga, the term '*bal*' meaning hair in Hindi.

Its significance lies in the fact that it is considered to be one of the four sacred places where Vaishno Devi is said to have taken refuge. Devotees visiting Vaishno Devi are expected to offer prayers at the Banganga temple and seek blessings from the goddess. The Banganga River flows peacefully, providing a calming atmosphere for the devotees.

Adhkuwari

After crossing the Banganga, at a distance of about 6 km and at a height of 4,800 ft above sea level, is the Adhkuwari Cave.

The Adhkuwari Cave is considered an important spiritual centre, and devotees believe that a visit to the cave can help in overcoming personal struggles and bring peace and tranquillity to the mind and soul. The trek to the cave is considered a challenging one, and the journey is said to symbolize the journey of life. The trek to the cave is considered a pilgrimage, and visitors show respect and devotion to the deity in the cave.

The cave contains a small temple dedicated to Vaishno Devi, where devotees offer prayers and seek blessings. The temple is surrounded by natural formations, such as stalactites and stalagmites, which add to the mystique of the place

At some distance from the Adhkuwari Cave is the next point of the pilgrimage at height of 6,200 ft called Sanjichhat. The final stop on the pilgrimage, where the devotees can access the three pindis, is called the Bhawan. Situated at about 5,200 ft, the holy Bhawan houses the sanctum sanctorum—the holy cave that is the ultimate destination of the yatris. Inside the holy cave, the goddess reveals herself in the form of holy pindis manifesting Mata in her three forms—Maha Kali, Maha Lakshmi and Maha Saraswati.

Sanjichhat

The Bhawan is also the place where all kinds of facilities and assistance are available for the yatris. As the final stop of the pilgrimage, along with all the important religious sites of Vaishno Devi, like the three pindis and the darshan of other important gods and goddesses, the Bhawan also has accommodation and catering facilities for the devotees as well as souvenir shops.

Most pilgrims prefer to take a bath before proceeding for darshan. In the olden days, pilgrims used to take a bath at the bathing ghat, with the water that flows from Mata's feet. With the passage of time, and particularly after the Shri Mata Vaishno Devi Shrine Board was vested with management responsibilities, new bathing ghats and many toilets and bathrooms have been constructed near the Bhawan. Attempts have been made to channelize the water from the holy cave to all these new bathing areas so that irrespective of where the pilgrims take a bath, they receive the cleansing effect of the holy water. The original bathing ghat has also been enlarged and developed.

Pilgrims are required to deposit all their belonging in the free cloakrooms, as nothing except cash and selected offerings are allowed inside the holy cave. All articles of general use, such as belts, wrist watches with leather belts, combs, pens, pencils, purses, handbags, etc., are prohibited. For the convenience of the yatris, the Shrine Board has organized free cloakroom facilities at many points in the Bhawan complex. These include the cloakrooms at Parvati Bhawan, Manokamna Bhawan and Gate No. 3. These cloakrooms can be used for depositing all leather and other goods, which are prohibited inside the holy cave.

After taking a bath at the bathing ghat or elsewhere, the pilgrims can reach Gate No. 1 skywalk. They are allowed inside the queue, which leads them eventually to one of the greatest moments of their lives, a darshan of the Divine Mother inside the holy cave in the natural rock form—the holy pindis.

While on the way to the sanctum sanctorum, one crosses a small patio-like structure (popularly known as Atka), on the right-hand side of which is a cave opening. This is the original cave leading to the holy pindis. In the olden days, the yatris used to reach the sanctum sanctorum through this cave. Nowadays, this cave is kept closed for a large part of the year. Since this cave is quite narrow, it takes several minutes for a single person to cross it and reach the sanctum sanctorum. Therefore, three new tunnels have been utilized to facilitate darshan for a larger number of pilgrims. The original cave is opened during the lean periods, on traditional festivals or for ritualistic occasions. Obtaining darshan through this cave is a different experience altogether, and pilgrims desirous of enjoying this divine bliss are well advised to plan their trip during the lean periods.

When one crosses the portion where the entrance to the original cave is located, one walks further through a corridor on which numerous bells stand suspended from the ceiling. After walking a few yards, one reaches a broad platform, where a life-size statue of the Mother Goddess is enshrined.

Upon entering the tunnel, one should observe silence and carefully move in the queue. At the end of the tunnel is a raised marble platform where the Divine Mother has revealed herself in a natural rock form known as the holy pindis. Pilgrims should refrain from shouting slogans of praise inside the tunnel and around the sanctum sanctorum. This disturbs other pilgrims who may be interested in concentrating on the darshan and descriptions given by the priests.

The priest sitting on the platform informs the pilgrims about these pindis, However, since the time for darshan is limited, one only gets a glimpse of the holy pindis and has to move further in order to keep the queue moving. There are no statues, pictures or idols inside. All along the way to and at the Bhawan, there are many photographs explaining the nature of darshan inside the holy cave. Yatris should observe these carefully since these are meant to guide them towards the final darshan in the holy cave.

One of the final stops for the devotees and pilgrims after reaching the three pindis is Bhairon Nath Mandir. It is a Hindu temple located in the vicinity of the Vaishno Devi Shrine. The temple is dedicated to Bhairon and is considered an important stop in the Vaishno Devi pilgrimage. The temple is located after a 3-km steep climb following the Bhawan. The Bhairon Nath Temple is considered a testament to the power of faith and devotion, and is visited by millions of devotees every year. The temple is an important stop along the Vaishno Devi pilgrimage, and those who visit it believe that by offering prayers, they will receive protection, blessings and peace for the rest of their journey.

Bhairon Nath Mandir

The temple is surrounded by lush green forests and rolling hills, providing a stunning backdrop for the temple. In addition to offering prayers, visitors at the Bhairon Nath Temple can also enjoy the scenic beauty of the area.

For the ease of travelling between the Bhawan and Bhairon Nath Temple, pilgrims can avail the facility of a passenger ropeway, which is functional between the two.

Vaishno Devi Bhawan, with Its Surrounding Environs

The Bhawan before the
Shrine Board Took Over Its Maintenance

## The Cave and Darshan

The holy cave is around 98-ft long and offers more than just the darshan of Maa Vaishno Devi. It is believed that close to 33 crore gods and goddesses have worshipped the Mother Goddess in the holy cave and have left their symbols inside, which can be seen and worshipped by the yatris on their pilgrimage. The most enduring and well-known symbols belong to Ganesha, Hanuman and Shiva. There is also the *dadh* (torso) of Bhairon Nath, whose main temple rests above the Bhawan.

Those who go for darshan through the old cave have to wade through water beyond this point. Around 23 ft after Launkra Beer, which is the lasting symbol of Hanuman's presence in the cave, on the left upper hand side, the roof of the cave flares out, and the entire weight of this cave appears to rest on the innumerable heads of Shesh Nag. Immediately below Shesh Nag is Mata's *havan kund*, and adjacent to it are the symbols of *shankh, chakra, gada* and *padam*.

Towards the middle of the cave, after various symbols of Hanuman, Ganesha, Shesh Nag, Shiva and Parvati are the famed holy pindis of Mata Maha Kali, Mata Maha Lakshmi Vaishno Devi and Mata Maha Saraswati, for which the yatri has made the pilgrimage. Next to the pindis is the full hand of the Mother Goddess, raised in the Varad Hast *mudra*, granting boons to the world. There are a few sources which believe that it was at this place where Sati's hand fell after her sacrifice for Shiva, thereby creating a Shakti Peeth. The darshan of the blessed hand, therefore, is just as important as the three pindis.

The ornamentation of the holy pindis was done gradually over a period of time. Various devotees offered jewellery, crowns, *chhatra*s, idols, etc. for the ornamentation of the holy pindis. The same ornamentation continued for several years and everything was kept practically untouched. Various idols and statues donated by kings and placed in the sanctum sanctorum were also visible immediately behind the pindis. This resulted in a cluttering of the sanctum sanctorum, and many pilgrims complained that the decorations and ornamentations tended to overshadow the holy pindis.

With the inception of the Shrine Board, it was decided to use a curtain behind the holy pindis, with fewer flowers for day-to-day ornamentation and decoration, in order to enable the pilgrims to have greater visibility and better darshan. The use of curtains and fewer flowers, coupled with efforts to inform and educate the pilgrims regarding the main darshan, led to positive results, and yatris reported having more satisfying and complete darshan.

Then, in 2000–01, on the persistent requests of many devotees and with the efforts of the Shrine Board, the entire ornamentation of the holy pindis was redone in pure gold. The platform around the holy pindis and the Atka were also renovated with white marble. The work was completed on 31 January 2001, and after puja and havan, the items of the ornamentation were presented at the lotus feet of the Divine Mother.

There are continuing requests from devotees who wish to offer ornaments, *chaddars* or other similar offerings in the holy cave. While smaller ornaments can be put into the jewellery box placed on the platform in the holy cave (along with sarees, *chola*s, *chunri*s [a red-coloured drape], etc.), larger ornaments may be deposited under proper receipt at the Office of the Sub-Divisional Magistrate, Room No. 8, Kalika Bhawan at the Bhawan or the Office of the Chief Executive Officer, Shri Mata Vaishno Devi Shrine Board, Central Office, Katra. The larger ornaments are then carefully stored in the strong room and used for ornamentation and decoration of the pindis on a rotational basis.

## *Bhaint* and *Prasad*

If the yatra budget is on the higher side and the devotee feels the need, they can always donate in cash or in kind and obtain a proper receipt for the same. The Shrine Board is a non-profit organization, and donations always help to create more and better facilities for all visitors and are used in larger public interest.

Computerized donation counters have been set up at various points in Katra and at the Bhawan, and devotees can offer cash, cheques or drafts and obtain computerized receipts on the spot.

Various counters have been set up by the Shrine Board to facilitate the pilgrims' donations. These counters are available at the Bhawan, Sanjichhat, Adhkuwari, Enquiry and Reservation office at Niharika Complex, Katra, and at the Central Office of the Shrine Board, Katra (Table 2). All these donation counters are fully computerized and manned by trained staff of the Shrine Board. Computerized donation receipts are issued to the devotees who make an offering or donation at these counters. These donation receipts can be preserved as a souvenir by the devotees. It also enables the devotees to claim income tax exemption on the donations made by them towards the Shrine. The details of these counters are given below.

**Table 2:**
**Location and Number of Shrine Board Donation Counters**

| Location | The Bhawan | Sanjichhat | Adhkuwari | Enquiry and Reservation Office, Niharika Complex, Katra | Central Office of Shrine Board, Katra | Kalika Dham/ Vaishno Devi Dham, Jammu |
|---|---|---|---|---|---|---|
| No. of donation counters | 3 | 1 | 1 | 1 | 1 | 1 |

Donation Centre

Donations in cash can also be dropped at the various *danpatras* located both inside and outside the holy cave, but in that case, the devotee is unable to get a donation receipt. More than 100 danpatras have been placed at various locations at Katra, en route and at the Bhawan. These boxes are regularly opened, and counting of the contents is organized under the careful watch of the senior functionaries of the Shrine Board.

The Shrine Board Building

FIVE

# The Shrine Board

The management of the yatra and the governance and administration of the Shrine is done by the Shri Mata Vaishno Devi Shrine Board, popularly called the Shrine Board. The Shrine Board was set up in August 1986, and under the provisions of the Jammu and Kashmir Shri Mata Vaishno Devi Shrine Act, 1988, it was formalized as its governing entity. The main objective of the Act is to provide better management and governance of the holy shrine of Shri Mata Vaishno Devi Ji and in 'endowments' including the appurtenant lands and buildings.

Under the provisions of the Act, the administration, management and governance of the Shri Mata Vaishno Devi Shrine and the shrine funds shall vest with a board, comprising a chairman and not more than 10 members. The lieutenant governor of the union territory of Jammu and Kashmir, by virtue of their office, is the ex-officio chairman of the Shrine Board. He nominates nine members for the Shrine Board at the policymaking level. The Shrine Board discharges its duties through a chief executive officer, who is assisted by the additional chief executive officer and various area heads and functional heads.

The establishment of the Shrine Board was necessary considering the poor state of things and the absence of facilities for the pilgrims back then. Before the Shrine Board, the pilgrims reached the holy town of Katra from all over India with devotion and faith in their hearts, but were often met with all kinds of hardships and insensitivity.

Ever since its establishment, the Shrine Board has continuously strived hard to provide all possible facilities to the devotees visiting the holy cave shrine of Shri Mata Vaishno Devi Ji. The efforts of the Shrine Board have been to make the yatra to the holy shrine of Shri Mata Vaishno Devi Ji a smooth and memorable experience. This has resulted in a tremendously increased number of yatris to the holy shrine of Shri Mata Vaishno Dev Ji. This has been possible due to the blessings of the divine and the all-round efforts of the Shrine Board. Presently, the Shrine Board is recognized as one of the major service-providing organizations in the country. Efforts are still afoot to further improve the facilities for the yatris and provide them state-of-the-art facilities in every sphere.

The takeover of the management of the holy shrine by the Shri Mata Vaishno Devi Shrine Board and the consequent efforts has resulted in several achievements, some of which are listed below.

## Track Development

Since the track and the cave are located in a mountainous region, convenience when it comes to walking and being able to access the cave and related holy sites are of primary concern to the Shrine Board. To this end, the entire stretch from Banganga to the Bhawan, covering a distance of over 12 km, has been laid with tiles, making the surface even and decreasing the difficulty of walking up the steep path. For the convenience of the pilgrims, another, alternate track measuring 5.5 km has been constructed; this track starts from Inderprastha (just below Adhkuwari) and reaches right up to the Bhawan.

Newer, Canopied Passageway Built by the Shrine Board, Which Protects Yatris from the Heat and Cold

Over 70 shelter sheds, covering a distance of nearly 4 km, have been constructed for rest and recuperation purposes. Fifty-two of these shelter sheds have been constructed on the main track, and 18 are on the alternate one. Pilgrims can relax and take rest at these shelter sheds, also called Vishram Sthals, where benches and other kinds of seating for resting are provided.

## Electricity, Water and Sanitation Availability

Both the main track and the alternate track have been well illuminated with approximately 1,800 LED street lights. More than 67 toilet blocks have been constructed along the routes at regular distances along the tracks and also in Katra.

Adequate water points, coolers and ATMs have been installed on the track to make clean drinking water available to the pilgrims and the yatris.

## Accommodation Accessibility

For the convenience of the yatris, a number of halls have been provided at Adhkuwari, Sanjichhat and the Bhawan. Pilgrims can rest here while waiting for their turn for darshan of the holy goddess or before proceeding further. These halls are available free of cost, but their availability is on a first come, first served basis. Pilgrims can also spend the night in these halls. Adjoining catering and toilet facilities have been made available here.

During days of heavy rush, free accommodation is also made available at Katra in the Niharika Complex. Accommodation in the form of sheds is also made available near the Yatra Parchi Counter II (YRC-II), adjacent to the New Bus Stand (Bus Stand No. II). Besides accommodation, blankets are also provided free of cost.

Accomodation at the Bhawan and in Katra for Yatris

Shri Mata Vaishno Devi Shrine Board also provides clean, well-maintained and very economical rented accommodation. This accommodation is available in Jammu (at Vaishnavi Dham, Kalika Dham and Saraswati Dham, near the railway station) and Katra (at Niharika Complex, Shakti Bhawan and Ashirwad Bhawan, situated at the bus stand). Another 700-bedded accommodation has been added at Trikuta Bhawan, which has been made available for the yatris. This building is situated near the YRC-II.

The available accommodation is in the form of rooms of various types, huts, suites and dormitories. Rooms, both air-conditioned and non-air-conditioned, are available. Dormitories are available in Katra and Jammu and at Adhkuwari and the Bhawan. In all the accommodation units provided by the Shrine Board, there is an additional facility of a hygienic, no-profit-no-loss *bhojanalaya*, along with a souvenir shop and a free cloakroom.

Accommodation for all Shrine Board guesthouses and dormitories can be booked (subject to availability) at the reception of these guest houses or at the Enquiry and Reservation office at Niharika Complex. Online booking is also possible through the Shrine Board's official website, www.maavaishnodevi.org, and the Mata Vaishno Devi app. For maximum chances of obtaining confirmed room reservations at various locations, devotees are advised to make the necessary bookings well in advance. In addition, since heavy rush is experienced on weekends and holidays, pilgrims are advised to plan their yatra on weekdays.

## Food and Refreshment Arrangements

Refreshments like biscuits, tea, coffee, milk, packaged water, etc., are available along the way at refreshment units of the Shrine Board. Nearly all of these units are located at carefully selected locations from where one can have a panoramic view of the valley. Therefore, they are also known as view points. There are a total of eight such view points, and six of these are located on the old track, one is located at the Katra Helipad, while one is located on the alternate track to the Bhawan. All the items offered at these view points are on a no-profit basis, thus ensuring proper quality and value for money.

The Shrine Board runs 16 bhojanalyas in all: four at Adhkuwari; two at Katra; seven at the main Bhawan; one at Bhairon Nath Temple; and two at Jammu. The bhojanalyas at the Bhawan run round the clock and serve a varied but traditional menu. In addition, two free langars, three buffet facilities, one bakery plant and one banquet kitchen are also operated by the Shrine Board for the yatris. The bhojanalayas serve multiple meals, bread, buns, hot and cold beverages, etc., while the view points only serve packed snacks and hot and cold beverages. Each outlet serves *satvik* food (without onion and garlic).

In addition, stretchers for patients and milk for infants are also available at view points. Most of the viewpoints are located at or near Vishram Sthals. Toilets and drinking water points are also located nearby. In brief, there are adequate opportunities for rest, rejuvenation and eating and drinking in and around the view points and the Vishram Sthals.

To further augment the catering facilities, the Shrine Board has taken many proactive measures by inviting reputed food chains to open their outlets on the track through an open competitive process. These reputed food chains include Sagar Ratna, Nathu's , Gulab, McDonald's, Dominos, Bikanervala and Coffee Day Global. Each outlet serves satvik food (without onion and garlic). There are a number of private establishments available on the track, but yatris are advised to ensure a fair price and quality of the goods being offered. In particular, yatris are strongly advised to desist from paying anything over the retail price printed on the packaged products.

## Access to Medical Facilities

The Shrine Board has, over the years, advocated for and invested in medical equipment as well as infrastructure along the pilgrimage route. Well-equipped medical units manned by capable professionals have been set up at Banganga, on Tarakote Marg, at Adhkuwari, Sanjichhat, Himkoti, the Bhawan and Bhairon Nath Temple.

At Sanjichhat, there is a 24-bedded, full-fledged

hospital with all facilities and emergency provisions, as some people, especially the elderly, might develop health complications due to high altitude. There are round-the-clock medical facilities, including an ICU, available at the Bhawan, with expert medical staff to take care of any and all emergencies. Besides, standby ambulances are also available for immediate shifting of patients to the referred hospital for specialized medical attention. There is also a goverment community hospital in Katra and a 300-bedded tertiary-care hospital of the Shrine Board about 9 km from Katra to attend to all medical needs of the pilgrims, the cost of which is covered by the Shrine Board.

## Presence of Bhaint Shops

Prasad/bhaint for offering to the deity can be purchased at a fair price from the Shrine Board-operated bhaint shops at the Bhawan. In addition, shops operated by private players (licensees of the Shrine Board) are also available.

## Provision of Souvenir Shops

For pilgrims who wish to carry with them mementos of the pilgrimage, the Shrine Board operates souvenir shops at the Bhawan, Himkoti, Spiritual Growth Centre, Katra bus stand and at Vaishnavi Dham (Jammu). The items that are offered by the devotees to the holy deity are available at the souvenir shops at nominal prices. Besides, exclusive items such as silver and gold coins of guaranteed purity having an impression of the holy pindis, diaries/calendar of the Shrine Board, laminated photos of the holy pindis, etc., are also available here. For online booking of souvenirs, please visit www.maavaishnodevi.org.

## Procuring Prasad

For the devotees desirous of prasad, it is made available in various denominations ranging from ₹100 to ₹2,100. The Panch Mewa Parsad is available to devotees at souvenir shops located at Darshani Deodi, Banganga, on Tarakote Marg and at the Bhawan. Besides, this facility is also available at stalls established at the helipad, airport and Niharika Complex and in Jammu, among others. The devotees can also book prasad through the Shrine Board's official website or the official mobile app.

## Establishment of Other Facilities

Due to the high altitude of Vaishno Devi, the pilgrimage route can get exceedingly cold. For the purpose of preventing the yatris from feeling the pinch of the weather, there are cloakrooms and blanket stores at all important locations. All these facilities are free of cost. Due to the popularity of Vaishno Devi, yatris and pilgrims belonging to all sorts of communities, ages, and identities visit the shrine throughout the year. Since the pilgrimage route is rather steep, especially near Sanjichhat and Adhkuwari, the facilities of ponies, mules, *pithus* and palanquins have been made available at fixed rates. For the pilgrims who are desirous of journeying to Bhairon Nath Temple, a passenger ropeway is functional between the two locations. This state-of-the-art imported ropeway complies with all essential safety standards. The ropeway ticket is available only on current basis through the ticketing counters established at the Manokamna Bhawan (no online/advance booking as of now). There is also a helicopter facility available on the Katra–Sanjichhat route and battery-car services on the Bhawan–Adhkuwari route.

Helipad at Sanjichhat

## Setting Up Other Services

Emergency services, such as banks, police stations and ATMs, have been made available at all important locations for the convenience of the pilgrims by the Shrine Board. The pilgrimage route itself is replete with shops selling toiletries, provision items, over-the-counter medicines, eatables, walking sticks, shoes, caps and raincoats. All shops have been licensed by the Shrine Board, and everything is sold at the retail price. Playing of regular announcements, recorded music, medical advisories, emergency public/individual announcements, live morning and evening Atka Aarti (audio), etc., is done through a multipurpose audio system functional 24 × 7. The system is integrated with 1,700 speakers and covers almost all strategic locations on the track. In addition, six hi-tech multipurpose video walls have also been installed at various prominent locations on the track. The video walls enable dissemination of real-time information with regard to early warnings of weather forecast, do's and don't's, live telecast of morning and evening aarti, awareness about various facilities and initiatives of the Shrine Board, etc.

There are many ways in which the devotees can assist the Shrine Board in their management of the pilgrimage. Some of them are listed below.

## Donations

Devotees can contribute to the Shrine Board's developmental activities by donating through the following modes:

1. At the donations counters of the Shrine Board at various locations (please do obtain a proper receipt for any such donation).
2. Via NEFT/RTGS/IMPS by visiting www.maavaishnodevi.org. (The donations made to Shri Mata Vaishno Devi Shrine Board are exempted from income tax under section 80G of the Income Tax Act.)
3. In addition to the above, devotees can also make donate approved items (donations-in-kind) at the stores of Shri Mata Vaishno Devi Shrine Board in Katra or at the Bhawan.

## Horizontal Growth Initiatives: Creation of Allied Institutions

### Shri Mata Vaishno Devi Narayana Superspeciality Hospital (SMVDNSH)

The SMVDNSH is a 300-bedded multi-specialty tertiary care hospital of the Shrine Board being operated in association with Narayana Health Group. The hospital provides quality healthcare at affordable rates to the people of Jammu and Kashmir. The pilgrims falling sick on the track and requiring specialized treatment are referred to this hospital for free treatment at cost to the Board.

## Shri Mata Vaishno Devi Gurukul, Charan Paduka, Katra

Shri Mata Vaishno Devi Gurukul (a fully residential institution affiliated to Sampurnanand Sanskrit Vishwavidyalaya, Varanasi) was set up by the Shrine Board in 2010 with the objective of promoting Vedic/Sanskrit education. The first session of the Gurukul started with 20 students admitted to Class 6th, while the higher classes as per need were progressively added. The present strength of students is 175. The Gurukul has won numerous laurels and recognitions in academic/co-curricular activities in a short span of time. The education at Gurukul is entirely free for students, and the Shrine Board bears all the expenditure in this regard. Besides, the Gurukul also regularly organizes free of cost workshops/refresher courses for pujaris of the entire Jammu region.

## Shri Mata Vaishno Devi College of Nursing (SMVDCoN)

The SMVDCoN was set up within the Shri Mata Vaishno Devi Institute of Medical Excellence (SMVDIME), Kakryal campus in 2016, with an intake capacity of 60 female students per year. This college offers a four-year BSc (Nursing) course and has student strength of 234 and a 100 per cent placement record so far.

The college, having approval of health and medical education department of the Government of Jammu and Kashmir as well as the Indian Nursing Council, is affiliated to with Shri Mata Vaishno Devi University.

## The Shrine Board's Sports Complex, Katra

With the aim of promoting physical activities and healthy lifestyle and inculcating the spirit of sportsmanship among citizens, particularly the younger lot, the Shrine Board created a magnificent sports complex in Katra in 2016. The complex, spread over 9.4 acres and inaugurated by the Hon'ble Prime Minister of India, boasts of splendid sports facilities such as a ground for track and field events; sports like football, cricket, judo and kabaddi; and impressive infrastructure for archery, gymnasium, lawn tennis, table tennis, shooting, basketball and volleyball, among others. The Shrine Board has in place a policy for providing strong institutional support in the shape of monetary awards to outstanding sports personnel. The players who have trained at this sports complex have attained numerous achievements in the national and international arena.

## Complaints and Suggestions

High priority is accorded by the Shrine Board's management of the devotees' complaints and suggestions. Complaint/suggestion boxes are available at various locations. Moreover, complaint registers are also available at all the important establishments. Feedback can also be given via email at feedback@maavaishnodevi.net.

## 24 x 7 Helpline

A dedicated single-window call centre (01991-234804) (callcenter@maavaishnodevi.net) is responsible for providing authentic information related to the pilgrimage. An emergency helpline number (01991-9797477777) is operational 24 × 7 and conspicuously displayed at prominent locations for the convenience of pilgrims. The pilgrims can also avail the services of announcement booths of the Shrine Board established at all important stations. By availing this service, the devotees can help the Shrine Board plan better for any emergencies that may arise.

Top View of Bhawan

SIX

# The Three-Day Pilgrimage

So now that all the information about Vaishno Devi and the rich history and mythology behind Shakti as well as the recent developments that the local governments along with the Shrine Board have undertaken has been provided, it is time to prepare and plan the yatra! There are a lot of things to be done and a lot of darshans to be made, so a detailed itinerary needs to be prepared for devotees and their loved ones to completely experience and sanctity of Vaishno Devi.

Ideally, a three-day itinerary or programme would allow devotees to visit all the important sites and pay their respects without feeling rushed. A three-day programme will be split into three parts, each covering a day. These are:

1. Arrival at Katra
2. Yatra from Katra to the Bhawan and beyond for darshans
3. Return to Katra

## Places of Tourist Interest in and around Katra Town

There are plenty of holy shrines in and around Katra apart from Vaishno Devi Bhawan itself. Some of them are associated with the legend of Maa Vaishno Devi, while some are temples and sites of historical importance in other ways. One can spend the remaining two days here, either before or after the darshan. All these places are connected by bus, and one can also avail of taxis to visit these places.

**Bhoomika Mandir:** An ancient temple situated just 700 m from Katra railway station, it is associated with the legends of Mata Vaishno Devi Ji. It is believed that Mata revealed herself to Pandit Sridhar at this place.

**Kol Kandoli Mandir:** This temple is situated in Nagrota Township, about 13 km from Jammu, on the way to Katra. Pilgrims desirous of visiting the temple are required to take a 4-km diversion from the National Highway at a place called Nagrota bypass. After darshan at this temple, they may head straight to re-link to the National Highway after 6 km.

**Deva Mai Shrine:** Located about 6 km from the Katra bus stand, this temple is believed to be the spot where Mata Vaishnavi meditated in her human manifestation during the early phases of Kalyuga. The temple is situated amidst a dense scenic forest.

**Baba Jitto Temple:** Baba Jitto was a staunch devotee of Mata. He sacrificed his life in an effort to get the rightful share of agricultural crops when it was denied to him by Jagirdar Bir Singh. Every year, a three-day *mela* (Jhidi Mela) is organized at this temple, which is attended by a number of farmers from Punjab, Haryana and Delhi.

**Nau Devi Cave:** This is a cave shrine located about 8 km from Katra on the Katra–Reasi road. The cave houses nine divine pindis representing nine forms of Maa Durga. There is a rivulet flowing on one side and a few natural water springs, making the area quite scenic. One has to crawl from the entrance of the cave before reaching the sanctum sanctorum.

**Baba Dhansar:** A magnificent cave shrine of Lord Shiva, situated about 13 km from Katra, it can be reached by taking a flight of around 100 stairs. Apart from the beautiful temple, what attracts tourists to this place are a number of marvellous waterfalls and lush greenery all around.

**Dera Baba Banda Bhadur:** A must-visit pilgrimage centre for the Sikhs, Dera Baba Banda shrine is located about 22 km from Katra. To reach the shrine, one has to take a diversion after travelling about 16 km on the Katra–Reasi road.

**Sula Park:** Sula Park situated at a distance of about 20 km on the Katra–Reasi road. Clear natural water springs, a rivulet nearby and greenery make this place a day-visit tourist attraction.

**Bhimgarh Fort:** This is a located on a hillock in the town of Reasi, about 26 km from Katra, and has a lot of historic value.

**Siar Baba Waterfall:** This is one of the biggest waterfalls in North India. It is situated in Reasi District at a distance of about 30 km from Katra, near the banks of Chenab River. The water descends here from an elevation of over 100 ft to present a scintillating view.

**Shri Shiv Khori Shrine:** The famous cave shrine of Shiv Khori is located in village of Ransoo in Reasi District, about 80 km from Katra. This cave abode of Lord Shiva is a venerated centre of attraction for pilgrims visiting Vaishno Devi. The holy cave is more than 150-m long and houses a 4-ft-high Svayambhu Lingum, which constantly bathes in a milky lime fluid dripping from the ceiling. The cave is full of natural impression, images of various Hindu deities and divine aura. Pilgrims are required to traverse a distance of about 3 km on foot or on ponies to reach the cave shrine. The shrine is managed by Shri Shiv Khori Shrine Board.

## Before Beginning the Yatra

Before beginning the yatra, there are a few things that one needs to be mindful of. Devotees must choose an appropriate date as per their convenience to undertake pilgrimage. Since Katra and Vaishno Devi are situated at an elevation and are in the northern reaches of the country, devotees must always keep the local climate and weather in mind before planning a pilgrimage, especially if they are travelling with children or the elderly. The holy shrine witnesses peak summer during April–June, heavy rainfalls during the monsoon months of July and August, extreme winter and heavy snowfall between December and February. Rest of the months have pleasant weather. The best time to visit for the best experience is either March–April or September–October.

They must also keep at least one reserve day to take care of unavoidable delays for unforeseen reasons such as bad weather, heavy rush, etc. After deciding on the dates, they must book various required facilities in advance such as the Yatra Access Card (RFID card), helicopter, battery car, accommodation, pujan slot, etc. This can be done through the official website of the Shrine Board or the Mata Vaishno Devi app. Advance booking of relevant facilities is strongly recommended to avoid any inconvenience. Katra town, the base camp for embarking on pilgrimage, is well connected to Jammu and rest of the country through air, rail, and road networks. The nearest airport is Jammu, which has daily flights coming in from all over the country. The railway has its network right upto Katra, and devotees can travel through various trains terminating at the Katra Railway Station. In addition, Katra is also connected to the rest of India through various modes of public and private road transport.

## Health and Safety Advisory

The pilgrims are advised to adhere to following useful guidelines related to their health and safety and to prevent avoidable mishaps:

1. Pilgrims suffering from heart, breathing or similar ailments are advised to begin the yatra only after

due medical check-up and advice. Cardiac, asthmatic and orthopedic problems are known to become aggravated due to the strenuous climb, especially at high altitude.

2. Pilgrims with relevant medical history and co-morbid conditions are also strongly advised against using the stairs.
3. Pregnant and elderly females must avoid moving alone on the track and are advised to use other modes of travel, including palanquins, to reduce the risks associated with on-foot travelling.
4. Pilgrims must avoid resting near landslide-prone areas and take due cognizance of sign boards in this regard, installed at various vulnerable locations of the track.
5. Do not smoke on the track. This is not only completely prohibited but could also be a trigger for a possible heart attack, stroke or other life-threatening ailments.
6. Avoid using routes closed for repairs or trekking through unspecified paths. This can prove to be extremely dangerous.
7. Cooperate with security agencies and enforcement staff, particularly at the time of rush, to safeguard against congestion and crowd formation.
8. Do not crowd anywhere. Instead, keep moving. In particular, at the Bhawan, after darshan, start the return journey as soon as possible.

9. Please do not ignore any of the following warning signs:
   a) Difficulty in breathing
   b) Chest pain
   c) Excessive sweating
   d) Giddiness/headache
   e) Blurry vision
   f) Palpitations
   g) Tingling sensation in arms or legs

In case any of the above warning sign(s) are observed, the pilgrim must seek immediate medical advice of qualified medical practitioner available at the nearest medical unit of the Shrine Board. This must be done without wasting any time and without resorting to self-medication. The medical units are conspicuously located at Banganga, Adhkuwari, Tarakot, Himkoti, Sanjichhat, Bhawan and Bhairon sectors and provide all essential services and medicines free of cost.

## Must Do's upon Disembarking in Katra

1. The most important activity that a pilgrim has to undertake on reaching Katra is getting registered for the yatra and obtaining a Yatra Access Card after verification from various yatra registration counters (Table 3). Devotees registered online can collect their Yatra Access Card from the yatra registration

counters by simply showing their registration number. The Yatra Access Card shall be issued to them from dedicated verification counters at Banganga and on Tarakote Marg on the way.

**Table 3:**
**Location of yatra registration counters**

| City | Location |
|---|---|
| Katra | Bus stand |
| | Railway station |
| | Tarakote Marg |
| | Serli Helipad |
| Jammu | Vaishnavi Dham |
| | Civil Airport |

2. The pilgrims are required to wear the Yatra Access Card throughout the journey for its auto-validation at various verification counters en route the Bhawan. The RFID card is issued by the Shrine Board *free of cost* and shall have to be returned at the exit locations at Banganga, on Tarakote Marg and on Serli Helipad. The securing of RFID card entitles the pilgrims to a free accidental death insurance cover of ₹5 lakh.
3. After obtaining the Yatra Access Card, the pilgrims are required to cross the first check post located at Darshani Deodi. No yatri without Yatra Access Card shall be allowed to undertake the pilgrimage to the holy shrine.

4. The yatris must plan to undertake the pilgrimage with minimum luggage (travel light). However, during winters, they need to carry warm clothing. All essential items, such as food, water, prasad, etc., are available en route at various locations and need not be carried.

Video cameras/drones are not allowed on the track.

## Mapping the Routes to the Holy Shrine

As mentioned earlier, in the past few decades, more than one route exists to reach the Bhawan for darshan, with a few of them even taking into consideration darshan to Bhairon Temple, which is above the Bhawan. According to devotees' programme and health, they can decide on any one of these routes, in addition to taking other means of transport to complete the pilgrimage.

1. Old/traditional route between Katra to the Bhawan (12.88 km), via Banganga, Adhkuwari, Hathimatha and Sanjichhat, is used by pedestrian pilgrims, ponies, pithus and palanquins.
2. Tarakote Marg between Katra and Adhkuwari (7.07 km) is used for pedestrians only.
3. Bhairon Marg between the Bhawan and Sanjichhat via Bhairon Temple (5.10 km)

4. Alternate track between Adhkuwari and the Bhawan via Himkoti (5.75 km)

The Various Routes to the Bhawan from Katra

## Undertaking the Pilgrimage

The actual time taken would largely depend on weather conditions, fitness of individual and the influx of pilgrims on a particular day. For helicopters, while it takes very less time to reach the Bhawan, yatris should be aware that due to safety guidelines as well as long queues, there can be a close to a three-hour wait between flights for going up and coming back down. However, following is the average expected time taken for going to and coming back from the shrine:

1. Helicopter: 4–5 hours
2. Ponies: 10–12 hours
3. Palanquins: 14–16 hours
4. Trekking: 14–16 hours

In case the battery car is used, the total pilgrimage time gets reduced by two hours.

These are the details regarding other modes of transport:

### Pony/Pithu/Palanquin

Reaching the Bhawan through ponies or palanquins is a very old and time-honoured tradition. Over the years, therefore, a rather sophisticated system for booking ponies and rides has developed. For prepaid booking of ponies, pithus and palanquins, a computerized integrated system is in place. Prepaid counters are established at strategic locations at Banganga, Adhkuwari, Sanjichhat, Bhairon Nath Temple and the Bhawan sectors. A robust system is also in place for the RFID tracking and e-surveillance of ponies, pithus and palanquins. The rates for availing the services are fixed and conspicuously displayed at all counters. All pony owners, pithus and palanquin operators are essentially required to carry identity cards.

## Helicopters

Two helicopter operators are presently providing heli-services in the Katra–Sanjichhat–Katra sector. Priority darshan is arranged for the pilgrims who have booked to and fro helicopter tickets. For detailed information regarding fare and ticket booking, the devotees may visit the official website of the Shrine Board or the official mobile app. Current booking can also be made by the pilgrims from the Shrine Board's current booking counter at Niharika Complex. It is subject to availability, and during most part of the year, only a limited number of slots are available. Therefore, it is strongly recommended that the devotees make their helicopter bookings online. The operation of helicopters is subject to fair weather condition, clear visibility of the range prescribed by the Directorate General of Civil Aviation and clearance by the Air Traffic Control.

Further, there are several fake websites/fraudsters that cheat the devotees by luring them towards helicopter tickets. The devotees are advised to remain cautious and beware of such unscrupulous elements. Any such complaint must be brought to notice of the police.

### Battery-Operated Vehicles

Pollution-free battery cars operate at fixed time slots on the Adhkuwari–Bhawan–Adhkuwari route. The pilgrims can book the battery-operated vehicle services either online through the Shrine Board's website or mobile app. They can also do so through current counters located at Inderprastha Bhojanalaya in Adhkuwari and Manokamna Bhawan at the Bhawan. Current booking is subject to availability (during most part of the year, only a limited number of current slots are available).

### Passenger Ropeway

For the pilgrims who want to visit the Bhairon Nath Temple, a passenger ropeway is functional between the two locations. This state-of-art imported ropeway complies with all essential safety standards. The ropeway ticket is available only on current basis through the ticketing counters established at Manokamna Bhawan. There is no facility of online or advance booking for now.

## Facilities for Yatris

To ensure a smooth, spiritual and peaceful yatra that allows all pilgrims to experience the holiness of Maa Vaishno Devi, the Shrine Board has added plenty of facilities and resources for the yatris' convenience. All Shrine Board-approved shops and stalls have their certificates posted on them for the sake of the pilgrims' satisfaction. All necessary facilities are completely free of charge for all yatris, whereas others cost a nominal amount.

## Accomodation

For temporary residence during the pilgrimage, a number of halls have been provided at at Adhkuwari, Sanjichhat and the Bhawan. Pilgrims can take rest here while waiting for their turn for the darshan of the holy goddess or before proceeding further. These halls are available free of cost but their availability is on a first come, first served basis. Pilgrims can also spend the night in these halls. Toilet facilities have been made available here.

For the convenience of the pilgrims, blanket stores, toilet blocks, bhojanalayas, catering units and a medical aid centre have been opened up in the near vicinity of these accommodations units.

During days of heavy rush, free accommodation is also made available in Katra at Niharika Complex.

Accommodation in the form of sheds is also made available near the YRC-II, adjacent to the New Bus Stand (Bus Stand No. II). Besides accommodation, blankets are also provided free of cost.

Shri Mata Vaishno Devi Shrine Board also provides clean, well-maintained and very economical accommodation on rent. This accommodation is available in Jammu (at Vaishnavi Dham, Kalika Dham and Saraswati Dham near the railway station), Katra (at Niharika Complex, Shakti Bhawan and Ashirwad Bhawan situated near the bus stand). Another 700-bedded accommodation, Trikuta Bhawan, is available for the yatris in Katra. This building is situated near the YRC-II. The Spiritual Growth Centre in Katra is also available for the yatris' accomodation. This building is situated near Asia Chowk (about 1 km from Main Bus Stand, Katra). Accommodation for the yatris is also available at Adkuwari, Sanjichhat and the Bhawan.

The available accommodation is in the form of rooms of various types, huts, suites and beds (dormitory accommodation). Rooms, both air-conditioned and non-air-conditioned are available. Dormitory accommodation is available in Katra and Jammu and at Adhikuwari Bhawan. In all the accommodation units provided by the Shrine Board, there is an additional facility of a hygienic, no-profit-no-loss bhojanalaya, besides a souvenir shop and a free cloak room.

All Shrine Board guest houses and dormitories can be booked (subject to availability) at the reception of these guest houses or at the Enquiry and Reservation counter at Niharika Complex. Online booking is also possible through the official website of the Shrine Board. For maximum chances of obtaining confirmed room reservations at various locations, devotees are advised to make the necessary bookings well in advance. In addition, since heavy rush is experienced on weekends and holidays, pilgrims are advised to plan their yatra on weekdays. Table 4 shows the rates of various rooms and beds with their facilities.

**Table 4:**
**Room Locations, Types and Tariffs**

| Location | Complex | Room Type | Tariff |
|---|---|---|---|
| Jammu | Vaishnavi Dham | Double Bedded, AC | ₹1,500 |
| | | Suite, AC | ₹2,000 |
| | | Dormitory (Per Bed Basis) | ₹150 |
| | Saraswati Dham | Dormitory (Per Bed Basis) | ₹150 |
| | Kalika Dham | Double Bedded, AC | ₹1,500 |

| Location | Complex | Room Type | Tariff |
|---|---|---|---|
| | | Dormitory, AC (Per Bed Basis) | ₹200 |
| Katra | Niharika Complex | Double Bedded, AC | ₹2,200 |
| | | Four Bedded, AC | ₹2,800 |
| | | Double Bedded, AC Deluxe | ₹2,200 |
| | | Four Bedded, AC Deluxe | ₹2,800 |
| | Shakti Bhawan | Dormitory (Per Bed Basis) | ₹150 |
| | Trikuta Bhawan | Dormitory (Per Bed Basis) | ₹150 |
| | Ashirwad Bhawan | Dormitory (Per Bed Basis) | ₹150 |
| | Spiritual Growth Centre | Double Bedded, AC | ₹1,900 |
| | | Suite | ₹3,300 |
| | | Dormitory, AC (Per Bed Basis) | ₹200 |
| Adhkuwari | Sharda Bhawan | Double Bedded | ₹800 |
| | Shailputri Bhawan | Dormitory (Per Bed Basis) | ₹150 |
| Sanjichhat | Mangla Bhawan | Double Bedded | ₹1,200 |
| | | Dormitory (Per Bed Basis) | ₹150 |

| Location | Complex | Room Type | Tariff |
|---|---|---|---|
| Bhawan | Main Bhawan Complex | Double Bedded | ₹2,400 |
| | | Four Bedded | ₹3,400 |
| | Vaishnavi and Gouri Bhawan | Double Bedded | ₹1,100 |
| | | Four Bedded | ₹1,600 |
| | | Six-Bedded Hut | ₹2,300 |
| | Manokamana Bhawan | Dormitory (Per Bed Basis) | Rs.150 |
| Extra Person Charges at Location | | | |

## Medical Facilities

To cater to the medical needs of the yatris, seven fully functional medical units with modern medical equipments are run by the Shrine Board at various strategic locations along the track to attend to any medical exigencies 24 × 7.

## Food

A langar facility is available at Tarakote on the Tarakote Marg. The donations from devotees are the mainstay of meeting the cost of operation of this langar. Besides the langar, a Prasad Sewa Counter is present at Sanjichhat, which serves cooked black *chana*, *halwa* and tea, and caters to yatris on a daily basis.

The Shrine Board operates various catering outlets in Jammu, Katra, and en route the Bhawan. These units serve wholesome and hygienic food and beverages to the devotees in a congenial environment and at reasonable rates. To add to the diversity of the food options, various private players including franchisees of reputed food chains have also been allowed to operate their catering units on the track. Buffet service is also available to devotees at Niharika Complex, Katra, and at the Bhawan.

### Water

For availability of drinking water to the yatris, water points and ATMs have been provided at various locations along the track. The water ATMs ensure availability of safe and seven-stage ultraviolet-filtered drinking water with 'warm', 'cold' and 'normal' options for the devotees.

### Sanitation

Clean toilet blocks and urinals points are available for the devotees at all prominent locations and all along the track at convenient intervals.

### Blanket Stores

The climatic conditions of the shrine area are such that the devotees would normally require blankets at night.

Free blanket stores are present at various locations where the devotees can get blankets for use without any charges, albeit against a nominal refundable security.

## Lockers and Cloakrooms

Free cloakroom facility is available at all major locations and complexes of the Shrine Board. As a general suggestion, pilgrims are advised to travel light to keep the use of this service to a minimum. Free cloakrooms are functional round the clock.

## E-Library

A digital library has been established at the Spiritual Growth Centre, Katra, with the aim to ease the difficulty of finding information from voluminous books. The e-library service is available for all knowledge seekers and is free of cost.

## Communication

Strong mobile connectivity has been made available by various telecom operators all along the track. To ensure that pilgrims carrying prepaid SIM cars, which do not function in Jammu and Kashmir, can stay connected, the Shrine Board has installed 24 x 7 STD/ISD/PCO booths at strategic locations. Yatris can also avail the yatri SIM, which is available in Katra.

### Online Services

The following online services can be availed by the devotees through the official website or mobile app of the Shrine Board:

1. Yatra Reservation
2. Donation
3. Room/Dormitory Reservation
4. Helicopter Reservation
5. Shradha Suman Vishesh Puja (SSVP) Reservation
6. Hawan Puja Reservation
7. Battery-Operated Vehicle Reservation
8. Prasad Booking
9. Atka Aarti

## On Reaching the Bhawan

After a long trek, or a tough ride on a pony or palanquin, the yatris finally reach the Bhawan. The cave and the holy mata's darshan await them. But there are still a few steps and instructions to be mindful of before the darshan, as there will be other pilgrims waiting for their own darshan.

Yatris would recollect that prior to the commencement of their yatra, they had obtained a yatra registration slip or parchi from the YRC located in Katra. This slip had been checked and stamped at

Banganga. The most important role of the slip is at the Bhawan, where it is revalidated and used to issue a group number. The group number is allotted at the Yatra Slip Counter located on the left-hand side immediately after the luggage check post. This group number would then determine the sequence in which the yatris would have their holy darshan and the duration for which they would have to wait before obtaining darshan. As has already been mentioned, the holy darshan in the cave of Shri Mata Vaishno Devi Ji are of natural rock formations called pindis with no idols or statues. Due to the narrowness of the cave and restriction on the number of people being able to pray inside the cave at any given point of time, darshan is regulated through a continuously moving queue.

On ordinary days or days of moderate rush, yatris can have darshan almost immediately after reaching the Bhawan. However, on days of heavy rush, especially during the peak months, one may have to wait for 9–10 hours.

## While Waiting

The devotees can start lining up in a queue as their group numbers are announced at Gate No. 1 after taking a bath at the bathing ghats or elsewhere. Immediately after a pilgrim's group number is called or displayed, he/she is ushered in through Gate No. 1 into the queue complex. This is a long corridor that opens first into two large waiting halls, one after the other and finally opens at the mouth of the holy cave.

During ordinary days, a pilgrim can enter Gate No. 1, and upon crossing the required distance, can reach the sanctum sanctorum in no time. But on days of heavy rush, one may have to wait inside the railings or the waiting room for some time before the queue ahead gets cleared. The Shrine Board has installed coloured television sets all along the queue corridor. These television sets relay a direct telecast of the holy cave and the holy pindis. Pre-recorded messages explaining the procedure of darshan are also relayed on these screens. Since the time available for darshan inside the holy cave is limited, yatris are advised to carefully watch the television sets and hear the pre-recorded messages. This will help them have proper darshan inside the cave.

In addition to the television sets, large back-lit, coloured photos of the holy pindis have been installed at various important locations. These are also meant to familiarize the pilgrims with the darshan inside the cave. Provision of urinals and drinking water has also been made in the waiting corridors.

The traditional offering to the goddess invariably comprises a coconut. However, for reasons of time and security, coconut offerings are not allowed to be carried by the pilgrims beyond a designated point.

Instead, at a designated point in the main waiting hall, pilgrims have to deposit their coconuts to the temple priests who then take responsibility for the rituals. The pilgrim is handed over a token and the offered coconuts can be reclaimed after darshan upon producing the token at the coconut prasad counter.

## The Darshan

Once the queue starts moving, the pilgrims can make their way to the holy pindis for darshan in an organized and disciplined way. They exit in the cave same manner as well.

Just outside the exit tunnel, towards the left hand side of the cave is the Amrit Kund. This comprises the water taps through which the water of the Charan Ganga, the sacred water from the feet of Mata, flows. Outside the exit tunnel and just beyond the Amrit Kund lies the prasad counter. The blessings of the Mother Goddess in the form of prasad pouches are handed over to the devotees by the temple priests.

### Types of Pujas

There are two types of pujas available at the holy shrine of Shri Mata Vaishno Devi Ji— Shradha Suman Vishesh Puja (SSVP) and Individual Puja—which can be booked online. The transaction status for the booking can be checked at the devotee zone by entering the username and password used for the booking. Once confirmed, the puja shall not be cancelled, postponed or preponed. The types of pujas are as below:

### *Shradha Suman Vishesh Puja*

This puja is for the devotees desirous of attending Aarti Darshan of the holy goddess. A package under the SSVP scheme is available for the devotees desirous of attending aarti darshan of the holy goddess. The details of the packages are as follows:

**Category A**

1. Aarti Darshan (inside the holy cave) for one adult along with a child below 10 years
2. One two-bedded AC room at Niharika Complex
3. One two-bedded room at the Bhawan
4. Maximum of three meals for one adult and one child in Katra/Bhawan
5. Prasad
6. Helicopter ticket/battery car ticket for one person
7. Prescribed donation amount: ₹26,000

**Category B**

1. Aarti Darshan (inside holy cave) for two adults along with two children below 10 years

2. One two-bedded AC room at Niharika Complex
3. One two-bedded room at the Bhawan
4. Maximum of three meals for two adult and two children to cost in Katra/Bhawan.
5. Prasad
6. Helicoper ticket/battery-car ticket for two persons
7. Prescribed donation amount: ₹48,000

**Category C**

1. Aarti Darshan (inside holy cave) for three adults along with two children below 10 years
2. One four-bedded AC room at Niharika Complex
3. One four-bedded room at the Bhawan
4. Maximum of three meals for three adults and two children in Katra/Bhawan
5. Prasad
6. Helicoper ticket/battery-car ticket for three persons
7. Prescribed donation amount: ₹71,000

**Category D**

1. Aarti Darshan (inside holy cave) for five adults along with two children below 10 years
2. One four-bedded AC room and one two-bedded AC room at Niharika Complex
3. One four-bedded and one two-bedded room at the Bhawan

4. Maximum of three meals for five adults and two children in Katra/Bhawan
5. Prasad
6. Helicopter ticket/battery-car ticket for five persons (subject to availability of service)
7. Prescribed donation amount: ₹121,000

**Please note:**

1. On auspicious days and Saturdays and Sundays falling between 15 March and 15 July, an amount of ₹35,000 per person is prescribed for SSVP.
2. No refund shall be allowed. If, after making payments, the yatri is not interested, the same shall be considered as a donation.

### *Individual Puja*

Every day, as a part of puja, a hawan is performed in the *yajnashala,* where the name, the gotra, etc., of the desirous person(s) shall be chanted and prayers will be offered for their welfare and prosperity. Yatris can visit the official site of the Shrine Board to book their individual pujas. Booking confirmation can be found on the website as well. In case of any booking-related queries, a mail can be sent to online@maavaishnodevi.org.

There are two categories under different prices for individual puja:

**1. Category A: Puja of ₹2,100**

The puja will be performed in the name of the person(s) for/by whom the puja has been registered; the devotee(s) will not be sitting in the puja. It can be booked for any day. The prasad will be sent through courier to the given address. A maximum of five names of a family can be given for the purpose, which shall be chanted during the course of the puja. The facility shall remain open for whole of the year.

**2. Category B: Puja of ₹11,000**

The puja can be attended by the devotee(s) themselves along with a maximum of four of their family members (five people in total). They need to report at Room No. 8 at the Bhawan before 8.00 a.m. to confirm the timings of the puja. Only advance booking will be allowed for this category.

**Please note:**

1. SSVP pilgrims are requested to collect their priority passes under the SSVP package from Enquiry and Reservation counter, Niharika Complex, Katra, by or before 12.30 p.m. to avail helicopter facility as part of the package.
2. The SSVP pilgrims are requested to reach the Katra helipad before 1.30 p.m. (for upward journey) and at Sanjichhat Helipad before

12.30 p.m. (for downward journey).

3. Any SSVP pilgrims breaching this timeline will not be entitled to fly in the helicopter as part of the SSVP package.
4. More than five persons shall not be allowed under the SSVP package unless they are all members of the same family, for which special and prior permission of the Shrine Board authorities is required.

## Other Darshans in the Holy Cave

As stated earlier, the darshan of 33 crore gods and goddesses are accessible to the devotees in the holy cave. It is also believed that during puja and aarti in the morning and evening, all these gods and goddesses arrive at the holy cave to pay their obeisance to the Mother Goddess.

At the entry of the holy cave, towards the left hand side, is the symbol of Vakra Tund Ganesh. Adjacent to the symbol of Lord Ganesh are the symbols of Surya Dev and Chandra Dev. Once inside the holy cave, one crosses over the dadh of Bhairon Nath, which is around 14-ft long. Due to the impact of the mighty blow of the Divine Mother, while the head of Bhairon Nath fell atop an adjacent mountain a couple of kilometers away from the holy cave, his body lay lifeless at the entrance.

After the dadh of Bhairon lies the Launkra Beer. Thereafter, one comes across Charan Ganga, the legendary river flowing from the feet of Mata. Those who go for darshan through the old cave have to wade through water beyond this point.

If one looks above, almost touching the ceiling of the cave are the symbols of five Pandavs, Saptrishis, *than* (udders or breast) of the divine cow Kamdhenu and Brahma–Vishnu–Mahesh and Shiva–Parvati. Three ft further ahead, at an elevation, the *khamba* that was gripped by the legendary devotee Prahlad can be seen. Diagonally below this, at the water level, is the *yantra* with innumerable mystical signs and symbols inscribed on it. Close to 22 ft beyond this point is the Sher ka Panja, the symbol of a lion, which is the mount of the Mata Vaishno Devi Ji. The distance from the entry point to the Sher Ka Panja is 59 ft. Around 13 ft beyond this, immediately above the head of the worshipper, is the symbol of the primary hood of Shesh Nag, which appears to be bearing the weight of the roof of the cave at this point. Six ft further ahead, on the left hand side, are the symbols of Shiva and Parvati.

About 13 ft beyond this are the holy pindis of Mata Maha Kali, Mata Maha Lakshmi Vaishno Devi and Mata Maha Saraswati. To the right of the holy pindis, on the upper side, the symbols of Lord Ganesh, Surya Dev, Chandra Dev and Goddess Annapurna can be seen. Slightly behind the holy pindis, on the right hand side, the symbol of the seated Sinh Raj (lion) is visible. A little ahead of it is the hand of the Mother Goddess in the Varad Hast mudra. Immediately opposite the holy pindis is the natural symbol of Lord Pashupati Nath.

Yatris may however note that most of these darshans are possible only if the original cave is used. However, owing to the heavy rush, usually, the new tunnels are used and the original cave is opened only during the lean seasons. Yatris desirous of having all the darshans are advised to formulate their programme to correspond with the lean seasons.

After this can be seen the symbol of Lord Hanuman called Launkra. Water gushes out of the base of the holy pindis and flows out of the holy cave. This gush of holy water is known as Charan Ganga, and the water of this stream is collected in small containers by the devotees and taken home. The same water is also channelized to the bathing ghat, and the devotees take a bath in this water before they join the queue for darshan of the holy pindis.

## Prasad and Bhaint

The traditional offerings to Mata include chunri (a red coloured drape), sarees, cholas, silver or gold ornaments, dry fruits, flowers, etc. No sweets are allowed inside the holy cave. Coconuts are also not permitted due to security considerations, and, hence, no coconuts are allowed to be broken anywhere near the holy cave, as is the practice at other temples. But being so intimately connected with the traditional offerings, they are not refused either. Pilgrims are required to deposit the coconuts at a counter in the main waiting hall before entering the holy cave and are given a token in return. They can reclaim their coconuts from a separate counter once they are out of the holy cave after darshan.

If one's budget is on the higher side, one can always donate in cash or in kind and obtain a proper receipt for the same.

All ornaments and jewellery offerings are to be deposited in the jewellery boxes kept in the sanctum sanctorum. Sarees, cholas, chunris, etc., are also accepted here. Devotees who wish to offer larger ornaments can also deposit the same at the Office of the Sub-Divisional Magistrate, Room No. 8, Kalika Bhawan at the Bhawan or the Office of the Chief Executive Officer, Shri Mata Vaishno Devi Shrine Board Central Office, Katra. The larger ornaments are preserved and offered at the feet of holy goddess on a rotational basis.

Outside the exit tunnel and just beyond the Amrit Kund lies the prasad counter. The blessings of the Mother Goddess in the form of prasad pouches are handed over to the devotees by the temple priests. Each prasad pouch comprises the mishri prasad plus a blessed coin, carrying the image of the holy pindis. In addition, *khazaana* (coins) are given to the devotees. This khazaana prasad is believed to bring good luck, and devotees are advised to keep it in their cash boxes, temples or other important places in their homes or establishments. The khazaana prasad has brought in prosperity and luck wherever it has been kept.

There are other blessed items too, especially the chunnis and the cholas, which are used for the holy pindis. Since the *vastra*s of the pindis are changed twice a day during aarti, the vastras that have been used once but are subsequently changed are offered as *aashirwad* (blessings) to the devotees. These are readily available at the souvenir shops run by the Shrine Board in Katra and at Adkuwari, Sanjichhat and the Bhawan. Gold and silver coins with the image of the holy goddess are also available. One may contact the officials of the Shrine Board for more details.

For yatris who wish to carry with them mementos of the great pilgrimage, the Shrine Board operates souvenir shops at the Bhawan, Sanjichhat, Adkuwari, Katra bus stand and Vaishnavi Dham (Jammu). Chunris, cholas, sarees and shawls that have been offered to the holy goddess are available at these souvenir shops at nominal prices. Pilgrims can obtain them and preserve them as souvenirs or can place them at the place of worship inside their houses.

Besides, other exclusive items available at the souvenir shops include, audio cassettes, CDs, various publications of the Shrine Board, laminated photos of the holy pindis, jute bags, bangles, chura, etc. Yatris may take notice that all these items are exclusively available at the souvenir shops of the Shrine Board and are not available at any of the private shops.

The Shrine Board has developed gold and silver coins of guaranteed purity. These coins carry an impression of the holy pindis and are offered at the feet of the goddess. These coins are available at the prasad counter just outside the holy cave and at all the banks at the Bhawan. The rates of the coins depend on the denomination chosen and the prevailing gold/silver rates.

# Aarti and Puja

SEVEN

# Aartis and Puja

The aarti of the goddess is performed twice a day, first in the morning just before the sunrise and second, in the evening immediately after the sunset.

The procedure of the aarti is a very sacred and lengthy one. The pujaris perform the aarti before the holy deity first inside the sanctum sanctorum and then outside the cave. Before its commencement, the pujaris perform Atma Puja, i.e., self-purification. Then the goddess is bathed in water, milk, ghee, honey and sugar. Thereafter, she is dressed up in a saree, chola and chunni and ornaments are endowed upon her. The whole process takes place amidst the enchantment of various *shlokas* and *mantras*. Thereafter, *tilak* (an auspicious mark) is placed on the forehead of the deity and *navied* (prasad) is offered to her. The pujaris perform pujas of various gods and goddesses, as it is a believed that during the aarti, all gods and goddesses are present inside the sanctum sanctorum. The *jyoti* (divine lamp) is lightened and then the aarti of the goddess is performed. After the whole procedure, the *thaal* that contains the lamp and various other items used in the aarti are brought outside the mouth of the holy cave, where the aarti of the goddess is performed again in the presence of yatris. The yatris who remain seated outside the holy cave when the aarti is performed inside the sanctum sanctorum keep listening to the *pravachan*s of head pandit. After the aarti outside the holy cave is over, the pujari distributes the prasad and *charanamrit* (the holy water) to the devotees. This whole procedure of aarti takes nearly two hours, during which darshan remains suspended. All the maintenance work required inside the cave is carried out during this time.

The various mantras chanted during aarti are given here. Only a general explanation of the mantras has been attempted. At the commencement of the aarti, the pujaris speak aloud the 108 names of the goddess, which are as follows (Table 5).

## Table 5:
## The 108 names of Mata

| Omsati | Daksha Yagya Inaashini | Sarva Asur Vinaashaa |
|---|---|---|
| Saadhavi | Aparnaa | Sarvadaanavghaatini |
| Bhav Preeta | Anek Varnaa | Sarva Shaastramavi |
| Bhawaani | Paaatlaa | Satya |
| Bhavmochani | Paatlaavati | Anek Shastra Hastaa |
| Aaryaa | Pattaambar Paridhaana | Anekaastraa Dhaarini |
| Durgaa | Kalmanjini | Kumari |
| Jayaa | Ameva Vikrama | Ek Kanya |
| Aadyaa | Krooraa | Kaishori |
| Trinetraa | Sundari | Yuvati |
| Shooldharini | Sarsundari | Yati |
| Pinaak Dharini | Van Durga | Apraudha |
| Chitraa | Maatangi | Praudah |
| Chandra Ghantaa | Matangmuni Pujita | Vriddhmaata |
| Mahaatapa | Braahmi | Balpradaa |
| Man | Maaheshwari | Mahodari |
| Buddhi | Eidree | Muktakeshi |
| Ahankaara | Kaumaari | Ghor Rupaa |
| Chittaroopaa | Vaishnavi | Mahaabalaa |
| Chittaa | Chaamundaa | Agni Jwalaa |
| Chitti | Vaaraahi | Raudramukhi |
| Sarvamantramavi | Lakshmi | Kaal Ratri |
| Sattaa | Purusha Kriti | Tapasvini |
| Satanandaswaroopini | Vimla | Naarayani |

| Ananta | Utkarshini | Bhandrakaali |
|---|---|---|
| Bhaavini | Gyaanaa | Vishnu Maaya |
| Bhaavya | Kriyaa | Jaloori |
| Bhavya | Nityaa | Shiv Dooti |
| Abhavya | Bhddhidda | Karaali |
| Sadagati | Bahulaa | Anantaa |
| Shaambhavi | Bahul Prema | Parmeshwari |
| Devmaata | Sarva Vaahan Vaahanaa | Kaatyaayani |
| Chintaa | Nishumbhashumbhahanini | Saavitri |
| Ratna Priyaa | Mahishasur Mardini | Pratyakshaa |
| Sarvvidyaa | Madhu Kaitabh Hantari | Brahm Vaadini |
| Daksha Kanyaa | Chanda Mundavinaashini | Sarva Shaastramayi |

The Atma Puja for self-purification is performed by chanting the following mantras:

> *Om apavitrah pavitro va*
> *Sarvavastham gatoapi va,*
> *Yah smrait pundarika aksham sa vahy*
> *Abhyantarah shuchih.*
>
> [Whoever contemplates upon Vishnu gets automatically purified, both mentally and physically.]

This is followed by *achman* (drinking of holy water after accepting it in the palm of the hand), which helps wash off the sins committed by action, thought and speech. The mantra runs as follows:

*Om keshavaya namah,*
*Om narayanaya namah,*
*Om madhavaya namah,*
*Om govindaya namah.*

[I bow to thee, Keshav, I bow to thee, Narayan, I bow to thee, Madhav, I bow to thee, Govind.]

This is followed by the chanting of the following mantra to welcome Lakshmi and applying tilak on the forehead of the pujaris.

*Om gandha dwaraam duraa dharshaam nityapushtaam karishinim,*
*Ishwarim sarva bhootaanaam taamihopahav yai shriyam.*

[Lakshmi, the omnipotent giver of prosperity, I respectfully welcome you to my home.]

In the next mantra, the pujaris pray to the goddess to grant them sound and robust health by chanting the following mantras:

*Om, ain, hridayaay namah,*
*Om vag mai aasyai astu,*
*Om nasor mai prano astu,*
*Om akshanor mai chakshur astu,*
*Om karnayor mai shrotram astu,*
*Om bahyor mai balam astu,*

*Om oorvor mai ojo astu,*
*Om arishtani mai angani,*
*Tanu stanva mai sahasantu*

[Oh Mother, keep my heart, speech, breathing, sight, hearing, strength and energy intact and disease free.]

After this the earth is worshipped in order to purify the place for sitting by chanting the following mantras:

*Om prithvi iti mantrasya meruprishta rishihi sutalam,*
*Chandah, koormo devtaa, aasan shodhanaya viniyogah.*
*Om prithvi tvayaa dhritaa lokaa devi tvam vishnuna dhritaa,*
*Tvam cha dhaaray maam devi pavitram kuru cha aasanam.*

[Oh Mother Earth, just as you hold the earth and Vishnu holds you. I beseech you to hold me and accept this seat that I am offering you.]

Thereafter, an *argha* (water containing a mixture of milk, rice, grass, etc.) is offered to Surya Deva while chanting the following mantras:

*Om ehi surya sahasraansho tejo raashay jagat patay, anukampaya maam bhaktya grihanaarghya divakar.*

[Oh Sun, master of the brilliant effulgence, please accept this argha that I am offering with complete devotion.]

This is followed by Deep Pujan (worship of the flame of the lamp) and Dhoop Pujan (worship of incense), which are performed by the chanting the following mantras:

*Om suprakaash mahaadeep sarvatra tamirapah,*
*Prasid mam govind deepo arghayah pratigrihyataam.*

[Oh Remover of Darkness, please accept my argha.]

*Om vanaspati rasod bhoot gandhaadya gandhuttamah,*
*Aargheya sarvadevaanaam dhoopoayam pratigrihya taam.*

[Please accept this essence of flora, which has such divine smell.]

This is followed by the Pratigya Sankalp (to resolve to fulfil a vow), which runs as follows:

*Om vishnur vishnur vishnu,*
*Om tatsadya brahmanoahini,*
*Dwitiya prardhe, vishnu pada,*
*Shri shwet varaah kalpe,*
*Vaivasvat manvantarey ashtaavinshati,*

*Tamey yugey kaliyugey,*
*Kali pratham charney,*
*Bhurlokey jambudweepey*
*Bharatvarshey bharatkhandey*
*Aaryar vartak deshey,*
*Vikram shakey baudhaavtaarey,*
*Amuk naam samvatsarey,*
*Shri suryey amukaayney,*
*Amuk maasey, amuk pakshey,*
*Amuk tithau, amuk vaasrey,*
*Amuk gotrotpannah,*
*Amuk sharma aham, shruti,*
*Smriti puraanokta phal praaptey,*
*Shri maataa vaishnavi devi*
*Siddhapeethey vishvakalyan ketavey,*
*Shri maataa mahaa kaali*
*Mahaa lakshmi mahaa saraswati*
*Shri maataa vaishnavi devi,*
*Pratah (saayan) kaaleen*
*Shodashopchaaren*
*Puja aham karishyey.*
*Tatraadau nirvighantaa sidhyartham ganapati puja nam cha karishey.*

[I shall worship Mata Mahakali, Maha Lakshmi and Maha Saraswati who are manifested in petrified rock form in the holy shrine of Mata Vaishno Devi Ji for the welfare of the world. I also vow to worship Ganapati (Ganesh).]

Once the Pratigya Sankalp is over, the *shringaar* of the goddess is removed, and ablutions are performed. While the goddess is bathed, mantras for *kalyan* (well-being) are chanted. These are known as Svasti Vaachan and are as follows:

*Hari om svasti na indro vriddha shravaah,*
*Svasti na pooshaah vishva vedaah,*
*Svasti na antarikshyo arishta nemi,*
*Svasti no brihaspatir dadhaatu,*

*Payah prithviyaam, payah aushadhishu,*
*Payo divya antarikshay,*
*Payodhaah paya svatih pradishah santu*
*mahayam.*
*Vishnor raatam asi,*
*Vishnoh shnapatrestho,*
*Vishno syoo ra si,*
*Vishno dhruvo asi vaishnavam asi vishna vetvaa.*
*Agnirdevataa vaato devtaa*
*Suryo devataa chandramaa devataa*
*Vasvo devataa rudra devataa,*
*Aaditya devataa maaruto devataa vishvedevah*
*devtaa.*
*Brishaspatir devatendro devataa,*
*Varuno devataa.*

*Om dhyau shantir antarikshe shaantih prithvi shanti raapah shaantir aushadhayah,*
*Shaanti vanaspatyah.*
*Shaanti vishve devah shaanti reva shaantih saama shaantiredhi sushantir bhwati.*
*Om vishvaani deva saviturduritani paraasuv yad bhadram tanna aasuva,*
*Imaa rudraaye tavase kapaddir*
*Nekshaya dwiraaye pravaraamahe matih yathaa shamsadwai padey*
*Chatushpadey vishvam pushtam graamey*
*Asminnaaturam,etantey deva savitur yagyam*
*Prahurbrihaspatye brahmaney teyn yagyamav teyn yagya patim teyn maamav*
*Mano jyotir jushatam ajasya brihas pati yagyam imam*
*Tano tvarishtam yagya samim*
*Mand dhattu vishvedevaah*
*Sa ihmadyantaamo pratishtha aishavey pratishthaa naam*
*Yagyo yatre teyn yagyen yajantey sarvam eva pratishthitam bhawati*
*Om devasyatvaa savituh prasave ashwino baahubhyaam pooshano hastaabhyaam.*

[All the mantras of Svasti Vachan pray for the well-being of the world and exhort that peace should prevail upon the earth and the universe. Oh

God, let your eight elements, namely, the heavens, space, earth, water, medicines, flora, Vishvay Deva and Brahma spread peace in the universe and ensure the well-being of all.]

After this, the goddess is bathed respectively with milk, curd, ghee, honey and sugar. As the bath with each of these is completed, the goddess is also bathed with water before commencing the bath with the next item. While these baths are going on the following mantras are chanted.

## Mantra for Bathing in Milk:

*Om payah prithviyaam paya aushadhishu payo divya antrikshe payodhaah,*
*Payasvatih pradishah santumahyam.*

[That which has been produced by the cow Kamdhenu, that which is the basis for all life, that which is also pure enough for being used in a yajna, such is the milk I am using to bathe you.]

## Mantra for Bathing in Water

*Om devasyatvaa savituh prasave ashvino baahu bhyaam pooshano hastaavhayaam*

*Asmin sannidhim kuru.*
*Om ganga sindhu saraswati cha yamuna godavari narmadhaa,*
*Kaaveri saryu mahendra tanya charmanvati vedika.*
*Kshipraa vetravati mahasur nadi khyataa*
*Cha yaa gandaki, purnaa purna jaley samudra sanhitaa kurvantu*
*Bho mangalam. Om mangalam bhagwan vishnu mangalam garud dhwaja,*
*Mangalam pundarikaaksha mangalam tano harih.*

[This is the mantra for bathing in water before entering the cave. This mantra is a part of the preparatory ritual that is well known at most yatras and melas where bathing is involved.]

After the ablutions are over, Lord Ganpati is worshipped by the chanting of the following mantras. It is to be noted that Lord Ganpati is always invoked when any auspicious act is to be performed:

*Om ganaa naantvaa ganpati hawaamahey priyaa naam*
*Tvaa priyapati havamahey hidhinaam tva nidhi pati*
*Hawamahey vaso mam,*
*Aham jaanigbbhardhamaa tvam*
*Jaasi ganey bhyo ganpati*

*Bhayasch vo namo namo, braatey bhyo braat patib hyascha vo namo namo,*
*Grihatseybhyo grihats patibhyasch vo namo namo,*
*Virupey bhyo vishvarupey bhayasch*
*Vo namo namah.*
*Om ganapatey namah.*
*Om sumukhah cha ek dantasch kapilo gaj karna kah,*
*Lambodarasch vikato vighna naasho vinaaya kah.*
*Dhumra ketu ganaar dhyaksho bhaal chandro gajaana nah,*
*Dwadash etaani naamaani yah pathait shranu yaad pai.*
*Vidyarambhey vivaahey cha praveshey nrigamey tathaa.*
*Sankatey cha ev*
*Vighnah tasya na jaayatey. Vakratund mahaa kaai koti surya samprab ha,*
*Nirvighnam kuru mey dev sarva kaaryeshu sarvadaa.*
*Om brahmaa muraari stripuraanta kaari bhaanuh shashi bhoomi suto*
*Vadhusch cha,*
*Gurusch cha shukra shani rahu ketavah sarvey grahaah shaanti karaa bhavan tu.*

[Oh Ganpati, we pray to you for overcoming all obstructions and for the welfare of our women, children and loved ones. We were born out of the wombs of our mothers whereas you emerged independently. Oh Lord with the Bent Trunk, Enormous Body and the Effulgence of a Million Sons, please remove all the difficulties that lie in the performance of my task.]

## Mantras for Beseeching Forgiveness for Sins and Faults

*Na mantram no yantram tadapi*
*Cha jaaney stutimaho*
*Na chaahvaanam dhyanam tadapi cha*
*Na jaaney stuti kathaah,*
*Na jaaney mudraa aaste tadapi cha*
*Na jaaney vilapanam*
*Param jaaney maatah tyad*
*Anusaranam klesh*
*Harnam.*
*Vidheyr gyaneyn dravinam virheynaa alastyaa vidheyaa shakya*
*Tvaat tav charan yoryaa chyutirbhut.*
*Tadey tat kshanta vyam janani saklo dwaarini shivey kuputro jaayatey kvachidapi*
*kumaataa na bhawati. Prithivyaam putraastey janani bahwa santi sarlaah*
*Param teshaam madhyey viral.*

*Taralo aham tav sutah,*
*Madiyo ayam tyaagah samuchitam idam no tav shivey*
*Kuputro jaayatey kvachidapi kumaata na bhawati.*
*Jagan maatar maatah*
*Tav charan sewaa na rachitaa na vaa datam devi dravinam api bhuyastav mayaa.*
*Tathaapi tvam sneham mayi nirupamam yat prakurushey kuputro jaayatey kvachidapi kumaata na bhawati. Parityaktaa devaa vividh vidh sewaa kul tayaa mayaa*
*Panchaashiteydhikam panitey tu vayasi, idaanim cheyn maatah tav yadi kripa na api bhavitaa*
*Niram lambo lambnodar jannani kam yaami sharnam. Shvapaako jalpaako bhawati madhupaako apamgiraa. Niraantanko ranko viharti chiram koti kankeyh,*
*Tvaa parney karney vishati manuvarney phalam idam*
*Janah ko jaanitey janani japniyam japvidyo.*
*Chitaa bhasmaa lepo garalam shanam dikpatdharo*
*Jata dhari kanthey bhujagpati haari pashupa tih, kapaali bhootesho bhajati jagdish ekaa padvim bhawaani tvatpaani grahan paripaati phalam idam.*

*Na mokshasya akaanshaa bhav vibhav vaanchha api cha*
*Na mey na vigyaan apekshaa shashi mukhi sukhechha api na punah.*
*Atah tvaam sanyaachey janani jananam yaatu mam veiy mridani rudraani shiv shiv bhawanni iti japatah.*
*Naa aaraadhitta asi vidhinaa vividhopchaareyh*
*Ki ruksha chintan papeirna kritam vachobhih, shyamey tvameyv*
*Yadi kinchan mayaa naathey dhatsey kripaam uchitamamba param taveyv.*
*Aapatsu magnah smarnam tvadiyam karomi durgey karunaaarnaveshi,*
*Nai tachhath tvam mam*
*Bhaavyeythah*
*Kshudha trishatrtaa janani smaranti*
*Jagdambn vichitra mantram kim paripurnaa karuna asti chenmayi,*
*Apraadh parampara param nahi maataa*
*Samupekshatey sutam.*
*Matsamah paataki naasti paapaghni tvatsamaa na he,*
*Evam gyaatva mahaadevi yathaa yogyam tathaa kuri.*

[Oh Mother, I am ignorant of either the ways in which you should be worshipped or the mantras that should be chanted in your praise. I do not even know how to meditate upon you. I am illiterate, lazy and poor. It is due to these defects that I often commit errors while trying to worship you. However, I know one thing for certain—if I persist in my endeavour to please you, I will be rewarded and you will remove all the sorrows that afflict me today. Oh, Mother, I am your child, and it does not behove you to discard me. For it is well known that even if a son may become an ungrateful wretch, his mother never forsakes him. Oh Mother, it is well known that if even a single word of the mantras chanted in your praise falls into the ears of the most wretched person he benefits beyond measures both spiritually and materially. And worshipping you regularly brings incalculable merit to your devotees. Oh Mother, it is well known that even Shankar attained his enviable status of Bhagwan only after you lent your helping hand by marrying him. Therefore, I would also like to spend my life in worshipping you rather than in seeking material pleasures. Oh Mother, even when a son commits one sin after another, his mother never rejects him. Instead, she accepts him and continues to love him. Oh Mother, there is no greater sinner than me and there is none who can forgive sins like you. So, I am throwing myself at your mercy. Please do whatever you think is appropriate.]

The following mantra is chanted while the goddess is dressed after the ablutions:

*Om yuvaah suvaasah pariveet aagaat sa*
*ushreyaan bhawati jaaye maanah,*
*Tandhi raasah kavaya unnyati swadhyo mansah*
*devyantah. Vastram samarpayaami.*
*Purush suktam*
*Harih om sahastra sheershaa purushah*
*Sahstra aakashah sahastra paat,*
*Sa bhoomi savatspritvaa tyatishthath dash*
*aangalam.*

[The Primordial *Purush* (Man) has innumerable heads, eyes and feet. He has enveloped the earth from all sides and even after that he has size to spare.]

*Purush eyved sarvavam yadbhootam yacch*
*bhaavyam, utaamrit tvasye shaano yadanney*
*naati rohati.*

[Whatever has occurred in the past and whatever will happen in the future is purush. He is the master of immortality and prosperity.]

*Etaa vaansya mahimaato jyaayaan shach purushah,*
*Paado asya vishwaa bhootaani tripaadasya amritam*
*divi.*

[This purush is incredibly great. The entire universe is adjusted in only one-quarter of his being and the remaining three-quarters are occupied by space.]

*Tripaad udddhrav udayat purushah*
*Paado syeha bhavat punah,' tato vishwan vyak*
*kraamatsa ashnaa nashney abhi.*

[Purush left three-fourths of his being for space, and with the remaining one-fourth of his being, he fashioned living and non-living things and spread them all around.]

*Tato virad jaayat viraajo adhi purushah,*
*Sajaato atyarichyat pashchaad bhoomi matho*
*purah.*

[Thereafter, a universal being known as Virad, who contained innumerable things, sprang out of the Primordial Purush. Virad, thereafter, produced another purush, who also had life. As soon as he came into existence, this purush fashioned himself into gods, men, etc. He then produced the earth and, thereafter, constructed a body.]

*Tasnnaadya gyaat sarva hutah sambhritam*
*prishdaa jyam,*
*Pashkunstaansh chakkrey vaayvyaa*
*Naaranya gramyashcchaye.*

[This purush then collected ghee mixed with curds and created the creatures that lived in the forests and in the sky.]

*Tasmaad yagyaat sarva hutrichah*
*saamaani jagyirey,*
*chhandaa asi jagyireyt a smaadya just smaad*
*jaayat.*

[Rig Veda and Sama Veda were produced by this purush. It was also he who created the Atharva Veda and Yajur Veda.]

*Tasmaadshva ajaayant yey key chobhyadatah,*
*gaavo ha jagyirey tasmaattsmaaja jaataa ajaavyah.*

[This purush created horses, asses, creatures with teeth on the upper and lower jaws, cows and goats and sheep.]

*Tam yagyam baharishi praukshann purusham*
*jaatam gratah.*
*Teyn devaa ajaayant saadhya rishyash cha yey.*

[The devas then worshipped this purush who was created before creation of the universe. Thereafter, the devas, the Prajapatis and the sages completed the yajna.]

*Yatpurusham vyad dhuh kati dhaa*
*Vyakalpayan,*

*Mukham kimsyaseetkim baahu kimru paadaa uchyetey.*

[When the Virad Purush was motivated to appear in person by the prayers of the devas, into how many parts was he divided! What were his face, arms, legs and feet called!]

*Brahmano asya kukham aaseed baahu raajanyah kritah,*
*Uru tadasya yadad vaishyah padbhyam shudro ajaayat.*

[The brahmins were born out of the face of this purush, the kshatriyas were born out of his arms, from the thighs and legs were born the vaishyas and the shudras sprung from his feet.]

*Chhandramaa manso jaatash chakshoh suryo ajaayat,*
*Shrotrad vayushcha praanash cha mukhaad agnir jaayat.*

[The moon was born out of his mind, the sun was born out of his ears and fire was born out of his mouth.]

*Nabyaa aaseedantariksha shirshno dyoh samvartat,*
*Padbhyaam bhumirddishah shrotraa tatha lokan ankalpayan.*

[From his navel was created space, from his head was created heaven, from his feet was created the earth and from his ears the four directions and the various worlds.]

*Yatpurusheyn havisha deva yagyam tanvat, Vasanto asyasi daajyam greeshma idhmah sharad dhvih.*

[After the devas were blessed with divine bodies, they performed a yajna with the materials that were fashioned out of the being of the purush. At that time, spring season acted as the ghee for the yajna, summer season acted as the fuel for the yajna and winter season acted as the mixture that is put as *homa* in the yajna.]

*Saptaasyaasan paridhyistrah sapt smidhah kritaah, Devaa yadya gyantanavaanaa abaghnan purusham pashum.*

[When the devas were performing this yajna with their minds in which they had transformed purush into animal form, the yajna had seven *paridhi*s and 21 *samidha*s. The seven paridhis included mantras like the Gayatri Mantra, and the 21 samidhas included the 12 months, five seasons, three worlds and the sun.]

*Yagyeyn yagyam yajant devaastaani dharmaani prathmaa nyaasan,*
*The naakam mahimaanah sachant yatra poorvey saad dhyaaah santi devaah.*

[The devas worshipped the purush with the yajna. It was this purush who was the first dharma. The worshippers (devas), therefore, attained *Swarg* or heaven. It is in this heaven that Brahma, who is an expert in fashioning the universe, lives along with the other devas.]

When the chanting of the Purush Suktam is over, the following mantras are chanted while sandalwood paste, rice grains and flowers are offered to the goddess.

## Mantras for Applying Sandalwood Paste

*Om gandha dwaaraam duraadharsha nitya pushtaam kareeshineem,*
*Eeshwareem sarva bhootaanaam taamihyop havyey shriyam.*
*Om tvaam gandharvaa akhanah tvaam indrah,*
*Tvaam brihaspatih,*
*Tvaam aushadhey somo raajaa vidvaan yaksham aadamuchayat.*
*Om shri khandam chandanam divyam gandhaadyam sumanoharam,*

*Vileypanam sursheshtha chandanam prati grihyaataam.*

[I beseech the all-powerful and master of all the riches Goddess Lakshmi to come here and kindly accept this divinely smelling sandalwood paste.]

## Mantras for Offering Rice Grains

*Om akshannam eemdant hyaav priyaa adhooshat,*
*Astaushat swabhanavo bipa na vishtthaya mati yojaanvindra tey haree.*
*Akshataan samarpyaami.*

[Oh Goddess, I offer to you rice grains that have been coloured with saffron and are fit for the gods. Please accept them.]

## Mantras for Offering Flowers

*Om ya phalineerya aphala apushpaa yaash cha pushpnee,*
*Brishaspati prasutaastaa no munchantvan hasah.*
*Om aushdheeh pratimo dhwam pushpvatih prasu varih,*
*Ashva iv sajitvareer veerudhah paar yishna vah.*

[I have brought these fragrant flowers for your worship. Kindly accept them.]

*Shri suktam*
*Om hiranya varnaam harineem suvarna rajat srajam,*
*Lakshmeem jaat vedo ma aavah.*
*Taam ma aavah jaat vedo lakshamee*
*Manap gaamineem,*
*Yasyaam hiranyam vindeyam gaam shvam purushaanaham.*
*Ashva purvaam rathmadhyaam hastinaad pra bodhineem*
*Shriyam devi muphavyey shrir maa devi jushaa tam.*
*Kaam so smitaam hiranya praakaaraa maar draam jwalanteem tripaam taarpayanteem,*
*Padmey sthitaam padma varnaa taami hop havyey shriyam.*
*Chandraam prabhaasam yashasaa jwalantim shriya lokey dev jushtaam udaaraam,*
*Taam padmaney imam sharanam aham prapadd yey alakshmirmay nashya taam tvaam vriney.*
*Aditya varney tapso adhijaato vanaspathstava virksho athbilvah,*
*Tasya phaaalaani tapasa nudantu maayantraa yaashcha baahyaa*
*Alakshmih.*

*Upetu mam devsakhah kirtish cha maninaasha,*
*Pradurbhooto suraashtrey asmin keertim vriddhim dadaatumey.*
*Kshutipa paasaamlaam yasyeshthaam lakshmmem naa shyaa mahyam,*
*Abhootim samriddhim cha sarvaa nirnud mey grihaat.*
*Gandha dwaaraam duraa dharshaa nitya pushtaam kareeshneem,*
*Eeshwareem sarvabhootanaam*
*Taami hop havyey shriyam.*
*Mansah kaamam aakutim vaachah satyamshimahi,*
*Pashunaam pupmannasya mayi shrih shreya taam yashah.*
*Kardameyn praja bhoota mayim sambhrav kardam,*
*Shriyam vaasaye may kuley maataram padmamaalineem.*
*Aapah srijantu snighdaani chikleet vas mey grihey,*
*Ni cha devim maataram shriyam*
*Vaasay mey kuley.*
*Aardraam pushkarineem pushtim pinglaam padmamaa lineem,*
*Chandraam hiranyamayeem lakshmeem jaat vedo ma aavah.*
*Taam ma aavah jaat vedo lakshee*

*manaagaamineem,*
*Yasyaam hiranyam prabhooteem gaavo daa*
*syoashvaan vindeyam purushaanaham. Yah*
*shuchin prayato bhutva juhuyaa*
*Daajyam anvaham,*
*Suktam panch darsh cha shri kaamah satatam*
*japety.*

[Oh Agni Deva, Sages Karabh and Chikleet, help me persuade Goddess Lakshmi to stay in my house. (Karabh and Chikleet are two of the four sons of Lakshmi. The other two sons are known as Anand and Shreet.) Oh Goddess Lakshmi, I beseech you to take up residence in my house and banish poverty and misery from it. Help me to befriend Kuber (the god of wealth) so that I can lead a life of luxury and happiness surrounded by my family and friends.]

## Mantra at the Time of Placing Garlands of Flowers

*Om maalya deenee sugandheeni maal tyaadeenee*
*vaye prabho,*
*Maya hootaani pushpaani poojaarth prati*
*grihyataam.*

*Dhyanam*
*On maata maka kaali*
*Om khadagam chakra gadeyshu chaap pa righaan*
*Chhulam bhushundim shrirah, shan kham sand dhatim karey stri naynaam*
*Dyootimaasya paad*
*Dashkaam sevey maha kaali kaam.*
*Yaamastau tasvapitey harau kamal jo hantum madhumkaitabham.*

[I worship Mata Kali whose help Brahma sought to kill the rakshas Madhu and Kaitabh. Mata Maha Kali carries a sword, a disc, a mace, a bow and arrow, a trident and a conch shell in her hands. Her body is adorned with divine ornaments and she has three eyes 10 faces and 10 feet.]

*Om maata mahaa lakshmi*
*Om akshastrak parshum gadeshu kulisham padmam dhanuh kundikaam*
*Dandam shaktimasim cha charm jaljam ghantaam suraabhaajanam,*
*Shulaam paash sudarshaney cha dadhteem hasteyh prasannannam.*
*Seyvey sairabhi mardineemih mahalakshmeem sarojsthitaam.*

[I pray to Mata Maha Lakshmi who destroyed Mahishasur. She is seated on a lotus flower and carries a rosary, a rope, a disc, a mace, a conch shell, a bell, a container for drinking honey and a shield.]

*Om maata maha saraswati*
*Om khanta shool halaani shankh musaley chakram dhanushayakam,*
*Hastaabjairadadhateem ghanaant vilaschitaanshu tulyaprabhaam.*
*Gauri deh samud bhavaam tri jagataam aadhaar bhootaam mahaa,*
*Poorvamatra sarswati manu bhajey shumbhaadi daitya ardineem.*

[Mata Sarswati carries a conch shell, a plough, a bow and arrow, a bell, a trident and a disc in her hand. She is the basis of the three worlds. She was created out of the body of Gouri and has a halo like that of the moon in winter months, I pray to her.]

## Mantras for Offering Incense

*Om vanaspati rasod bhooto gandhaadyo gandh uttamah,*
*Aaghreya sarva devaa naam*
*Dhoopoayam prati grihyataam.*
*Om dhoorsi dhoovra dhoovra*
*Vantan dhoovrav tam yo asmaan.*
*Devaanaamasi vahintamah*

*Sasnitamam prapitmam jushtatam*
*Devhootamam om dhupaay namah.*

[This is a mantra for offering incense. It is uttered when *agarbattis* (incense sticks) are lit. The mantra articulates a request for the goddess to accept the offering of the divine smell that is being extended.]

## Mantra for Worshipping the Flame of the Lamp

*Om suprakash mahaa deep sarvatastim rapah,*
*Prasid mam govnd deep arghyah prati grihyataam.*
*Om agni jyotir jyotir agnih swaahha suryo jyoti jyotir suryah swaahaa.*
*Agnir varcho jyotir varchah*
*Swaaha*
*Suryo varcho jyotir varchah*
*Swaahaa.*
*Jyotis suryah suryo jyotih swaahaa.*
*Om deepaey namah.*

[This mantra is uttered while lighting the lamp and worshipping its flame when the lamp is being offered to the goddess.]

## Mantra for Naivaidya

*Om naabhya aasid antriksha sheershano dyoh samvartat.*
*Padbhyam bhoomir dashah shrotraa tathaa lokaam lokaam akalpayan.*
*Naivaidyam nivedyaami.*
*Om praanaaya swaahaa om aapnaaya swaahaa.*
*Om samaanaya swaahaa om udaanaay swaahaa.*
*Om vyaanaaya swaahaa.*
*Naivaidyantey punar aachmaneeyam Samarpayaami.*

[He who produced space from his navel, Heaven from his head, Earth from his feet and the directions from his ears and also created the various worlds, please accept my offering.]

## Mantra for Aarti

*Om idam havih prajanaanam mey astu dashveerah sarv gana swastaye,*
*Aatmsni prajaasani pashusni*
*Loksanya bhay sni.*
*Agni prajaam bahulaam mey karo tavnam payo reto asmaasu dhatta.*
*Aa raatri paarthivah rajah*

*Piturampraayi dhaammih.*
*Divah sadaa asi brihati vitishthhas*
*Aatvesham vartaty tamah.*

[May this 'Havi' be the producer of innumerable powerful and brave creatures. May this 'Havi' give strength to the soul, to the people, to the animals, indeed to the entire world. May this Havi benefit me too and spread happiness and well-being all around.]

## Guruji ki Vandana

*Om prathmey guru ji ki vandana*
*Dwiteeya aad ganesh.*
*Thriteeya simraan shaarda*
*Mere karaj karo hamesh.*
*Aanandi aanand karo kalyaani kalyaan.*
*Aathh prahar chausathh ghari deyo charnan daa dhyaan.*

[This is a prayer to the Mother Goddess and all her forms, beseeching her blessings and praising her divinity.]

## Aarti of Mata Vaishno Devi

*Om jaya shri sunder lalitey mahaa*
*Jaya shri sunder lalitey*
*Chakropari raajatkaameshwar sahitey*

*Om jai dev jaya dev*
*Om saa vindu guna kono pari raajat.*
*Vasukoney mahaa raajat mahaaraajat.*
*Tad upari dash ko na dhwaj shuddh chatur dwaaree.*
*Om jai deva jaya deva.*
*Matindeyndu kadaatal bhooshit guna rajasey,*
*Mahaa raajat mahaa raajat,*
*Tadupari trirek nirmit shobhit manu rajsey,*
*Om jay dev jaya dev.*
*Shri chakropari raajat manu vin mahaa tanutey*
*Mahaaraajat mahaaraajat*
*Neeranjan sah tvanjey param safal lalitey,*
*Om jay deva jai deva.*
*Tvamm maam paalay nityam.*
*Tavaan maam palay nityam*
*Mahaaraajat mahaaraajat*
*Trikutua jagdambey.*
*Om jai dev jai dev.*
*Om jai shri sunder lalitey.*
*Mahaa jai shri sunder lalitey.*
*Shri chakro pari raajat kaameshwar sahitey,*
*Om jai dev jai dev.*
*Om aartirkyam samar pyami.*
*Om onkaaram vindum sanyuktam nityam dhyay*
*Antiyoginah kaamdam mokshadam chaev*
*Onkarraay namo namah.*

[The one who is constantly worshipped by the sages and who grants salvation to all, I salute you.]

*Om shankha madhya sthitam toyam bhraamitam devyopari,*
*Anga lagney manushyanam brahm*
*Hatya dikam hareyt.*

[Whoever touches you, who is at the heart of the seashell, sheds off even the most heinous sins.]

## Mantras for Offering Flowers

*Om yagyen yagya maya jant*
*Devaastaani*
*Dharmaani prathmaa nyaasan.*
*The naakam mahimaanah sachant yatra*
*Poorvey saadhyah santi devaah.*
*Om mahaa devi cha vidmahey Vishnu*
*Patni cha dheemahi,*
*Tanno devi pracho dayaat.*
*Om vakra tundaaye vidmaehey ek dan taaye dhee mahi,*
*Tanno danti pracho dayaat.*
*Om naa naa sugandhi pushpaani ritu kaalo bhawaanee cha,*
*Pushpaanjali maryaadatta grihaan parmeshwari.*

[I have heard of the Goddess from the teachers and the scriptures and have tried to mediate upon her. I now beseech the same Goddess Vaishnavi to motivate me to mediate upon her. I have heard of Lord Ganesh from the teachers and scriptures and have mediated upon him. I pray to Lord Ganesh to motivate me to mediate upon him. I have prepared this collection of flowers by procuring flowers that grow in this season from different places. Oh Great Goddess, kindly accept my offering of flowers.]

## Stuti

*Hey maat meri, hey maat meri hay maat meri,*
*hey maat meri.*
*Kaisee yeh deyree lagaai hai durgey,*
*Hey maat meri, hey maat meri.*
*Bhav saagar mey giraa padaa hoon*
*Kaam aadi grah sey ghiraa padda hoon.*
*Moh aadi jaalon mey jakda padda hoon.*
*Hey maat meri hey maat meri.*
*Na mujh mey bal hai na mujh mey vidya,*
*Na mujh mey bhakti na mujh mey shakti,*
*sharantumhaari giraa pada hoon, hey maat meri,*
*hey maat meri.*
*Na mera koi kutumb saathi, na hi meraa shareer*
*saathi,*

*Aap hee ubharo pakad ke bahen,*
*Hey maat meri hey maat meri.*
*Charan kamal kee naukaa*
*Banaa kar, main paar hoongaa khushi manaa*
*kar, yam dootaon ko maar*
*Bhagaakar, hey maat meri hey maat meri.*
*Sadaa hee tere gunoon ko gaaoon,*
*Sadaa hee tere swaroop ko dhyaoon.*
*Nit prati tere gunon ko gaaoon,*
*Heymaat meri hey maat meri.*
*Na main kissi kaa na koi meera.*
*Chhayaa hai charo aur andhera,*
*Pakad ke jyoti maa dikhaao rasta,*
*Hey maat meri hey maat meri.*
*Sharan pade hain hum tumhari,*
*Karo yeh naiyaa paar hamari,*
*Kaisee yeh deri lagaayee hey janani,*
*Hey maat meri hey maat meri.*
*Om tvamev maata cha pita tvamev*
*Tvamev bandhushcha sakhaa tvamev,*
*Tvamev vidya chadravinam tvamev*
*Tvamev sarvam mam dev dev.*
*Om shaantaakaaram bhujag shayanam*
*padmanaabham suresham,*
*Vishwaadhaaram gagan sadrisham meghavarnam*
*shubhaangam.*
*Shri lakshmikaantam kamalnayanam yogibhir*

*dhyaangamyam,*
*Vandevishnu bhavhayaharam*
*Sarvlokey eknaatham.*
*Om achyutam keshavam raam*
*Naaraayanam krishan. Daamodaram,*
*Vaasudevam harim.*
*Shridharam maadhavam gopikaa vallabham*
*jaanaki naayakam shriraam chandram*
*bhaje.*
*Om harey muraarey madhu kaitabharey govind*
*gopaal mukund kishorey,*
*Gyanam pradehi sharnam pradehi vidya pradehi*
*bhagwan namo stutey.*
*Sanche darbar ki jai*
*Sachiyan jotanvaali maataa teri sadaa hee jai.*
*Panchphoolan raani maataa teri sadda hi jai.*
*Sarvatra da bhalaa karan vaali maataa teri sada*
*hi jai.*
*Saare sansaar vich shanti deyn vaali maataa teri*
*sada hi jai.*
*Launkara veer thakur teri sadaa hi jai.*
*Bol saanchey darbar ki jai.*
*Durgey smrita harsi bheetim shesh jantoh,*
*Swastheyhsmrita matimateev*
*Shubham dadaasi.*
*Daaridrya dukhbhayahaarini katvadanya,*
*Sarvorkaar karanaaye sada*
*Ardrachitta.*

[Oh Goddess Durga, you remove the fear of all those who think of you and grant them a sharp mind. You are always busy doing good for others.]

*Sarva mangala maangalye*
*Shiveysarvaarth saadhikey,*
*Sharnaye trayambakey*
*Gauri naaraayani namostutey.*

[Oh Narayaani, Oh Shivi, Oh Gauri, you fulfil the desires of all. I pray to you.]

*Sharnaagat deenaart paritraan paraayaney,*
*Servasyarti harey devi naaraayani namostutey.*

[You who are perpetually endeavouring to protect the weak and the poor and remove their misery. Oh Narayani, I pray to you.]

*Sarvasvaroopey sarveshey*
*Sarvshakti samanvietey,*
*Bhayebhyah traahi noodevi*
*Durge namostutey.*

[Oh Goddess Durga, please protect us from all kinds of fear. Oh Omnipotent Durga, I pray to you.]

*Rogaan shoshaan*
*Pahansitushtarushtatu*
*Kaamaan saklaan bhishtaan,*
*Tvaam aashritaanaam na*

*Vipannaraanam.*
*Tvaamaashritaahya shraytaam prayaanti.*

[Oh Goddess, when you are pleased, you remove all ailments, and when you are angry, you destory everything that a person desires. However, those who come to you for sanctuary never have to confront any catastrophe. Instead, such people secure enough merit to provide shelter to others.]

*Sarva badha prashmanan trailokya*
*syakhileshwari,*
*Evamevmev tvayaa kaaryam sma dveri*
*visaashnam.*
*Sarvaa baadha vinirumk to dhan dhaanya sutaan*
*vitah.*
*Manushyo mat prasaaden bhavishyati na sansha*
*yah.*

[Whoever listens to the story of the goddess during the great puja that is organized in the winters succeeds in overcoming all obstacles and is blessed wealth and progeny.]

*Jyanti mangalaa kaali bhadra kaali kapaalinee*
*durgaa kshamaa shivaa dhaatree swaahaa*
*svadhaa namo stutey.*

[Oh Goddess, you who are known by the names of Mangala, Kali, Bhadra Kali, Kapalinee, Durge,

Kshama, Shivaa, Dhatri, Swahaa, Swadha, I pray to you.]

*Dehi saubhaagyam aarogyam dehi dvisho jahi.*

[Oh Goddess, bless me with good fortune, good health, good looks, success and fame.]

*Videhi devi kalyanam videhi parmashriyam,*
*Rupam dehi jayam dehi yasho dehi dvisho jahi.*

[Oh Vaishnavi, you are the very basis for the world. You have mesmerized the world. When you are pleased with someone, you ensure his salvation from the cycle of life and death.]

## Prayer Beseeching Forgiveness

*Apraadh sahastraani kriyantey harnisham mayaa,*
*Daaso yamiti maan matvaa kshamasv parmesh wari.*

[I commit thousands of sins everyday. Oh Goddess, please think of me as your slave and pardon my crimes.]

*Aa vaahanam na janaami na janaami visarjanam,*
*Pujaam chaev najanaami.*

[I know not how to call you, nor how to appease you. Nor do I know how to worship you. Oh Goddess, please forgive me.]

*Mantra heenam kriya heenam bhakti heenam sureshwaree.*
*Yat pujitam mayaa devi pari poorna tadastu mey.*

[Oh Sureswari, this puja that I have performed has been done without the chanting of proper mantras. Forgive me. I entreat you to make this puja successful.]

*Apraadh shatam kritvaa jagdambeti chohret.*
*Yaam gatim samnaapotinataam brama dayah suraah.*

[He who seeks sanctuary in you even after committing hundreds of crimes and calls out your name 'Jagdambikay' attains the kind of salavation, which is not easily available to even the devas.]

*Saapraadho asmi sharanam praaptah tvaam jagdambikey, iddaaneem anukampayo aham yathechhasti tathaakuru.*
*Kaameshwari jaganmaatah sachiddanand vigrahey,*
*Grihaanaar chamim aam preetya praseed parmeshwari.*

[Oh Goddess Parmeshwari, please pardon whatever excesses or shortcomings I have committed as a result of ignorance, loss of memory or misunderstanding. Oh Goddess, please accept my prayers. I beseech you to shower your blessing upon me constantly.]

*Guhyaatiguhya goptree tvam grihaa naasmatkritam japam, tvatprasaadaat sureshwari.*

[Oh Goddess, you are the protector of the most secret of things. Please accept my prayers and grant me salvation.]

EIGHT

# Initiatives by the Shrine Board

Shri Mata Vaishno Devi Shrine Board has been looking after the administration and management of the holy shrine since 1986. The shrine is frequented by 8–10 million pilgrims every year. To accommodate this volume of tourism, various facilities are provided and upgraded by the Shrine Board on a regular basis so that pilgrims can have a hassle-free yatra experience.

## SHRI MATA VAISHNO DEVI CHARITABLE SOCIETY

In furtherance to its efforts, the Board has recently constituted Shri Mata Vaishno Devi Charitable Society under the Societies Registration Act, 1860, which is headed by Hon'ble Lt Governor, Jammu and Kashmir. The society manages SMVDNSH, a 300-bedded super specialty hospital; SVMD College of Nursing; and SMVD Gurukul, a school of Sanskrit-based Vedic learning. The society has now been registered by the Ministry of Corporate Affairs for receiving funds under corporate social responsibility (CSR). To contribute under CSR/general donation, please visit www.maavaishnodevi.org.

## SHRI MATA VAISHNO DEVI SPORTS COMPLEX

Recognizing the significance of competitive physical activities for promoting health as well as inculcating team spirit and sportsmanship, a quality sports facility has been set up in Katra. A multipurpose sports complex, built at a cost of more than ₹10 crore, was inaugurated by Hon'ble Prime Minister of India on 19 April 2016.

Throughout the year, sports activities and events are organized in the sports complex, which includes a magnificent ground for track and field events for sports such as football, cricket, judo and kabaddi. Moreover, the complex has also state-of-the-art infrastructure for archery, gym activities, lawn tennis, basketball, volleyball, table tennis and shooting.

To provide training to stimulate nationally recognized sports, Paralympic sports and Olympic sports, the SMVDCS has engaged professional coaches in various disciplines. Players trained at the sports complex have won numerous laurels by claiming significant achievements at national and international levels.

## SHRI MATA VAISHNO DEVI COLLEGE OF NURSING

In July 2016, the SMVDCoN was set up in the SMVDIME premises in Kakryal. The SMVDCoN, built at a capital cost of more than ₹25.61 crore, offers four-year BSc (Nursing) course. It has an intake capacity of 60 students per batch. To bridge the gap between the income (fees received from students) and the expenditure of the college, suitable grant-in-aid is provided every year by the Shrine Board as per the college's need.

The SMVDCoN is affiliated to Shri Mata Vaishno Devi University and approved by Department of Health and Education, Jammu and Kashmir, and the Indian Nursing Council. Further, the college has the recognition of Jammu & Kashmir State Paramedical and Nursing Council as well. So far, three batches have graduated from the college, with an impressive 100 per cent placement. Besides core academics, the college organizes a string of co-curricular activities for the overall growth of students.

In an attempt to further consolidate its presently impeccable reputation, the college is contemplating to bring in more initiatives for holistic growth. These include enhancement of the intake capacity of BSc (Nursing) from 60 to 80 students per year; starting a new master's programme in Applied Sciences in Healthcare Quality and Patient Safety; and acquiring an autonomous status through accreditation with the National Assessment and Accreditation Council (NAAC). The college shall soon be making suitable additions in its physical and administrative infrastructure to cater to the augmented activity status.

## SHRI MATA VAISHNO DEVI GURUKUL, CHARAN PADUKA, KATRA

Shri Mata Vaishno Devi Gurukul was set up in 2010 with the objective to impart Sanskrit-based Vedic knowledge and to produce adequately qualified and skilled professionals in the fields of Sanskrit and religion. The first session of the Gurukul started with admission of 20 students in Class 6th. Subsequently, higher classes were progressively added, in line with the annual progression of students. This fully residential institution provides education, boarding, books, uniforms, etc., to the students by the Shrine Board free of cost.

The Gurukul of the Shrine Board is affiliated to the Central Sanskrit University, New Delhi, from the academic session 2022–23. (It was earlier affiliated to Sampurnanand Sanskrit University, Varanasi). Mahamadleshwar Shri Swami Vishveshvaranand Giriji Maharaj, Hon'ble Member of the Board, is also the present chairman of the governing council of SMVD Gurukul.

The students are admitted in Class 6th through an entrance examination followed by an interview. Presently, there are 164 students studying in Gurukul (Class 6th to Shastri Part III). Besides Sanskrit subjects, the students are taught contemporary subjects as well, and are also encouraged for extracurricular activities for their overall growth. Consequently, the students of Gurukul have won laurels in academic as well as extracurricular arenas.

## SHRI MATA VAISHNO DEVI NARAYANA SUPERSPECIALITY HOSPITAL, KAKRYAL

Considering a certain void in the availability of reasonable healthcare facilities in and around the Katra region, the Board conceived a super speciality hospital in Kakryal (a village adjoining Katra) at a cost of more than ₹300 crore, funded entirely by the Shrine Board. It was completed in the year 2016 and inaugurated by the Hon'ble Prime Minister of India on 19 April 2016. The SMVDNSH is being managed by the Board (Authority) in a public–private partnership with Narayana Vaishno Devi Specialty Hospitals Private Ltd (concessionaire) in the terms of provisions of a Concession Agreement.

The SMVDNSH provides splendid medical services across more than 20 diverse specialties to a large number of patients through cash and schemes (Ex-Servicemen Contributory Health Scheme, Central Government Health Scheme, Employees' State Insurance, Ayushman, etc.). The hospital has a capacity of about 325 beds with plans for increasing it to more than 500 beds and providing matching infrastructure/medical equipment to take care of additional footfalls. All the cost of augmentation of infrastructure will be met by the Board.

Simultaneous with the commissioning of the SMVDNSH, the Board also came up with a medical support policy of paying for specified extent of treatment to various beneficiary groups including pilgrims, landowners (whose land was acquired by the Board), employees of the Board, students of the Gurukul and College of Nursing and other poor and needy persons in need of financial support. Since operation of the hospital in 2016 till October 2022, the Board has incurred expenditure in excess of ₹40 crore in its provision of medical support to various beneficiaries.

NINE

# Frequently Asked Questions

## Q. How do I reach Katra?

Katra is located at a distance of 50 km from Jammu, and Jammu is connected with the rest of the country by road, rail and air. It is connected with Delhi and Srinagar by air.

Jammu is also connected to all the major cities of the country by rail. Indian Railways operates a large number of trains with air-conditioned and ordinary coaches to and from the city every day. Taxis are available at Jammu airport and railway station for transporting the pilgrims to Katra. The Jammu and Kashmir State Roadways Transport Corporation operates a large number of buses at regular intervals from the Jammu railway station to Katra. Private deluxe buses also operate between the railway station and Katra. Besides these, there is also a regular bus service between Jammu and Katra from the General Bus Stand in Jammu. Buses leave for Katra after every 15 minutes from the General Bus Stand. The bus service commences at 5.30 a.m. and concludes at 8.30 p.m. every day.

### Q. What should I do before proceeding for the yatra from Katra?

Before proceeding to the Bhawan for darshans, please ensure the following:

1. Obtain a yatra parchi from the YRC at the general bus stand in Katra. The yatra slip is free of cost and can be obtained between 6.00 a.m. and 10.00 p.m.
2. Do not carry video cameras, as they are not allowed on the track.
3. Book a room for the Bhawan, Sanjichhat or Adhkuwari from Enquiry and Reservation, Shakti Bhawan, Niharika Complex, and collect your papers to be shown at the location for which the room is booked.
4. Do not carry too much jewellery or cash with you.

### Q. Can I avail accommodation at the Bhawan and in Katra? How?

In Katra, besides the accommodation offered by the Shrine Board, private hotels, dharamshalas and the government accommodation are available. However, at the Bhawan, Sanjichhat and Adhkuwari, the Shrine Board is the only agency through which accommodation can be arranged. The accommodation offered by the Shrine Board is broadly of three types, namely, free accommodation, rented rooms and rented dormitories. Free accommodation provided by the Shrine Board is in the form of big halls available in Katra and at Adhkuwari, Sanjichhat and the Bhawan. For this type of accommodation, advance reservation is neither required nor available. Rented rooms and dormitories are available to the yatris against advance reservation. The advance reservation of rooms and dormitories is done at the enquiry and reservation section of the Shrine Board against cash payment, cheques and draft. The address is:

Enquiry and Reservation
Shakti Bhawan, SMVDSB
Katra-182 301
Phone: 01991-234053

For current reservation of accommodation, subject to availability, besides the central office of the Shrine

Board, a yatri can also contact the Shrine Board's offices at the locations where the accommodation is sought.

### Q. What is the procedure to make donations?

The Shrine Board depends entirely on the donations of pilgrims for carrying out its developmental programmes. Therefore, pilgrims are requested to donate generously. Donations made to the Shrine Board are exempt from income tax under section 80G of the Indian Income Tax Act. The donations can be either put directly in the donation boxes kept at different locations or made at specific donation counters against proper receipt. A jewellery box has also been placed at the sanctum sanctorum, and the gold and silver jewellery offered by the pilgrims is put in it. The Shrine Board also accepts donations by cheques and drafts payable to Shri Mata Vaishno Devi Shrine Board in Katra or Jammu. For this purpose, the cheque or draft can be sent at the following address:

Shri Mata Vaishno Devi Shrine Board,
Central Office, SMVDSB
Katra-182 301
Phone: 01991-232167

## Q. What are the essential things I need to carry before starting for pilgrimage?

Please ensure that you are carrying the following things with you when you proceed to the Bhawan for darshan:

1. The yatra slip
2. Room reservation papers, if any
3. One or two spare garments as per season/ weather
4. A torch and an umbrella.
5. Canvas shoes if undertaking the pilgrimage on foot

## Q. How and where can I hire ponies and palanquins?

For hiring the registered ponies, pithus or palanquins, a yatri is required to contact the contractors' offices at the Bhawan and Adhkuwari or in Katra. The rates for these are approved by the government, and for convenience, the same can be cross-checked from the signboards installed by the Shrine Board along the track at prominent locations. Before engaging ponies, palanquins or pithus, a yatri is required to note down the registration number of the person(s) so engaged for reference. In case of any problem with the contractor's office, the field offices of the Shrine Board can also be contacted.

### Q. How is the weather in Katra and at the Bhawan, and what kind of garments do I carry?

At the Bhawan, during the summer months, the weather is moderate, whereas in the winter season, sub-zero temperature is experienced. The monsoon season witnesses heavy rainfall. Temperature at the holy shrine normally ranges from 30°C in the summers to about -5°C during the winter. Since the Bhawan experiences heavy snowfall during the months of December, January and February, it can become extremely cold during winters. Pilgrims are advised to carry heavy woollen clothing with them if they wish to undertake the yatra during winters. In fact, heavy woollen clothing should be carried by pilgrims from October to March. April is an unpredictable month. The weather can turn quite cold if it rains. So, it is advisable to carry light woollens during this month. May to September are very pleasant months when even cotton garments are sufficient.

### Q. What is the procedure for darshan?

Before commencing on the yatra from Katra, pilgrims are supposed to get themselves registered at the yatra registration counter at the Katra bus stand. The yatra slip is available free of cost from 6.00 a.m. to 10.00 p.m. During rush period, when the yatris in Katra exceed the clearing capacity at the Bhawan, the pilgrims are held back in Katra and issued a temporary waiting group, which is later converted into final slip on first come, first served basis. The yatra slip obtained in Katra is required to be verified first at Banganga's slip check post and then at the Bhawan's slip check post. On arriving at the Bhawan, a fresh group number is allotted to the pilgrims, which is stamped on the yatra slip collected from Katra. This group number is essential for darshan at the Bhawan.

**Q. I have an aged relative. Will it be convenient to bring them for darshan? What assistance is available?**

It is absolutely convenient for the devotees of all age groups right from young children to elderly people to come for darshan, as adequate facilities, like catering, porters, accommodation etc., are available in Katra, at the Bhawan and en route. For people who cannot do the yatra on foot or ponies, palanquins can be engaged.

**Q. Are adequate catering arrangements and milk for the children available en route?**

Yes, the Shrine Board has made adequate catering arrangements in the form of bhojanalayas and view points, where, besides the other items, milk is available for children. There are private shops that provide various eatables at different locations as well.

## TEN

# Precautions for Yatris

As mentioned previously, there are various ways of completing the journey to Mata Vaishno Devi—through ponies, helicopters or even electric vehicles—that have been introduced recently. The most common way still, however, is walking, as it is believed that walking to the shrine is auspicious and looked upon favourably by Vaishno Devi, who took the route herself on foot.

Like any trek, the yatra to Mata Vaishno Devi has its own challenges. Over the years, a lot of facilities and infrastructure has been added to ease the discomfort of the yatris, such as LED lighting, paved paths and the aforementioned electric vehicles and helicopters. But since the entire journey covers close to 13 km, there are still some basic precautions that need to be taken while undertaking it. They are as follows:

1. Plan the trek with respect to the time and weather. While there are plenty of covered sheds yatris can rest in on the way, it is recommended to start the yatra either early in the morning or early in the evening. The trek, while more convenient now than before, is still arduous, especially around noon.
2. Always keep the yatra parchi on hand at all times. It is issued at the Katra base camp and will be needed at various check points on the route to the shrine. It is necessary to gain admittance to the cave.
3. There are two main routes to reach Mata Vaishno Devi: the traditional trek from Katra and the newly constructed Bhawan–Bhairon ropeway. As per the yatris' fitness level and preferences, either can be opted.
4. Undertaking the trek requires a moderate level of physical fitness. While planning the trek, the devotees should engage in regular exercise and prepare their bodies for the trek. In case of any pre-existing health conditions, medical consultation is important.
5. Beware of any scams or fraudulent activity. A lot of pilgrims visit Maa Vaishno Devi every year, and there are unscrupulous organizations or persons that try to take advantage of innocent yatris. The Shrine Board has not entered into any agreement

with any third party regarding tours or special access to the cave or the pindis. The only darshan and puja available to yatris are the ones outlined on the Shrine Board website and in this book. Please do not fall for any such schemes and report them to the Shrine Board if any such organizations are operating within Katra.

6. Carry comfortable trekking shoes, lightweight clothing suitable for the weather, a small backpack, a water bottle, a raincoat or umbrella, sunscreen, sunglasses and a hat. It is also recommended to bring some energy snacks for the trek.
7. Stay hydrated throughout the trek by drinking water at regular intervals. There are several drinking water facilities available along the trail. Carry energy drinks or electrolyte sachets to replenish lost minerals.
8. Follow the designated trekking path and obey safety guidelines. Stick to well-lit areas, especially if trekking at night. Stay with respective groups and avoid venturing alone into isolated areas.
9. Please uphold the sanctity of the pilgrimage and avoid loud dresses, vulgar language or offensive talk or gestures. The yatra is a journey of faith. Please do not treat it as a picnic or a vacation.
10. Respect the sentiments of co-pilgrims.
11. Cooperate with the security agencies for security checks.

12. Please avoid resting near landslide-prone areas.
13. Refrain from smoking, chewing tobacco and betel leaves, spitting, littering, playing cards, etc. Consumption of liquor, intoxicants and non-vegetarian food is strictly prohibited.
14. Keep the environment clean. Do not litter the hill slopes. Throw the disposables in dustbins only. In particular, minimize use of plastics.
15. Avoid carrying too much cash, jewellery and valuables. Take proper care of your belongings and beware of pickpockets and petty thieves.
16. Do not trust strangers with your belongings. Deposit all excess baggage in the cloak rooms.
17. Do not eat anything offered by strangers.
18. Beware of suspicious persons and unclaimed articles and report them to the security personnel.
19. Do not encourage begging. Begging is strictly prohibited.
20. Obtain a cash receipt for any cash paid at the Shrine Board outlets.
21. Avoid using routes closed for repairs. This can prove extremely dangerous.
22. Yatris with high blood pressure or heart or asthamatic problems must seek clearance from their doctors before starting the journey.
23. Yatris with any kind of medical problems are strongly advised against using the stairs.
24. Sticking posters, writing on the walls, mutilating or

damaging the property is a legal offence punishable with both fine and imprisonment.

25. Do not crowd anywhere. Keep moving.
26. Video shooting en route is prohibited. Please leave all video cameras in Katra.
27. Self-service is the motto at all Shrine Board outlets. Hence, no room or table service is provided.

Finally, always remember to chant:
Jai Mata Di!